'*Psychoanalytic and Socio-Cultural Perspectives on Women in India: Violence, Safety and Survival* offers both a distinctly psychoanalytic view of the trauma and resilience of women in India and an interdisciplinary consideration of their religious, familial, societal situation historically and currently. Horrifying abuse of Indian women is juxtaposed with clinical and social documentation of women's fierce public insistence on equality and justice. This presentation of the impacts of fundamentalism, patriarchy, and severe socio-cultural endangerment constitutes an inspiring and scholarly contribution to clinicians' and social scientists' work with underprivileged women world-wide.'

- **Harriet Wolfe, M.D.** *is President-elect of the International Psychoanalytical Association and Clinical Professor of Psychiatry and Behavioral Sciences at the University of California San Francisco*

'*Psychoanalytic and Socio-cultural Perspectives on Women in India*, another remarkable book produced by COWAP, one of the most relevant IPA committees, shows how psychoanalysis is able to shed light on a complex reality, both psychological and social, hand in hand with other disciplines. The life of women in India, so well depicted in this excellent book, both in their inner lives and in the culture they live in, is a remarkable contribution to our growing awareness of the feminine, its glories and difficulties, and once again illustrates the development of psychoanalytic understanding of human mind and body in different cultures. I strongly recommend this book and congratulate its authors.'

- **Cláudio Laks Eizirik**, *IPA Past President, Professor Emeritus of Psychiatry, Federal University of Rio Grande do Sul, Brazil, Sigourney Award, 2011*

Psychoanalytic and Socio-Cultural Perspectives on Women in India

This important book provides a bridge between psychoanalytic perspectives and socio-cultural issues to shine a spotlight on the experiences of women in India today.

Women's well-being and security has often depended upon their gender positioning while other binaries like rural-urban, class, and caste have also played a crucial role globally and especially in India. Historically, women have been subjected to various forms of oppression that include sex selective abortions, domestic violence, bride burning for dowry, and acid attacks. Threats to women's security have recently increased with progressive polarization and hardening of socio-political and cultural ideologies. This book assesses how women's lives are impacted by these social and cultural conventions and stigmas, including ideas around motherhood, religion, intimacy, and femininity itself, and the psychological implications these have. Topics include the seduction of religion, motherhood in contemporary times, intimacy and violence, and fundamentalist states of mind in the clinical space. While the book echoes a regional specificity, it simultaneously resonates a backdrop of global change of affairs that has its impact on ideological freedom and the concept of inclusivity in terms of gender, race, culture, and politics across the world. For this comprehensive perspective, the effort is to create a platform of authors comprising psychoanalysts, social scientists, scholars from the liberal arts discipline, as well as social activists.

In a country where women have been historically subjected to both psychological and physical oppression, this timely and original book will interest a range of scholars interested in gender, mental health, and contemporary Indian society, as well as clinicians in the field.

Paula L. Ellman, Ph.D., ABPP, is a training and supervising analyst in the Contemporary Freudian Society, Washington, DC, and the Washington Baltimore Center for Psychoanalysis. She is the overall chair of the IPA Committee on Women and Psychoanalysis, chair of the IPA Intercommittee on Prejudices and Racism, is on the editorial board of the International Journal of Psychoanalysis, and is a board member of the North America Psychoanalytic Confederation (NAPsaC).

Jhuma Basak is a training analyst of the Indian Psychoanalytical Society. She is the representative of the 4th IPA region in the Committee on Women & Psychoanalysis, and member of the IPA Humanitarian Organization Committee.

Dr. Gertraud Schlesinger-Kipp is a psychologist and psychoanalyst and, since 1989, has owned a private practice in Kassel. A member of the German Psychoanalytical Association (DPV, IPA) and a full member of the IPA. Schlesinger-Kipp has been a training analyst and supervisor since 1998, a member and consultant of COWAP since 2002, and is chair of migration and refugees subcommittee.

Psychoanalysis and Women Series
Series Editor
Frances Thomson-Salo

For more information about this series, please visit: https://www.routledge.com/Psychoanalysis-and-Women-Series/book-series/KARNACPWS

Psychoanalytic and Socio-Cultural Perspectives on Women in India

Violence, Safety and Survival

Edited by
Paula L. Ellman, Jhuma Basak,
and Gertraud Schlesinger-Kipp

Routledge
Taylor & Francis Group

LONDON AND NEW YORK

First published 2022
by Routledge
2 Park Square, Milton Park, Abingdon, Oxon OX14 4RN

and by Routledge
605 Third Avenue, New York, NY 10158

Routledge is an imprint of the Taylor & Francis Group, an informa business

British Library Cataloguing-in-Publication Data
A catalogue record for this book is available from the British Library

Library of Congress Cataloging-in-Publication Data
Names: Ellman, Paula Lisette, editor. | Basak, Jhuma, editor. | Schlesinger-Kipp, Gertraud, 1952- editor.
Title: Psychoanalytic and socio-cultural perspectives on women in India : violence, safety and survival / edited by Paula L. Ellman, Jhuma Basak, Gertraud Schlesinger-Kipp.
Description: Milton Park, Abingdon, Oxon ; New York, NY: Routledge, 2021. |
Series: Psychoanalysis and women series | Includes bibliographical references and index. |
Identifiers: LCCN 2021002083 (print) | LCCN 2021002084 (ebook) | ISBN 9780367182823 (hardback) | ISBN 9780367182830 (paperback) | ISBN 9780429060502 (ebook)
Subjects: LCSH: Women--India--Social conditions. | Women--India--Psychology.
Classification: LCC HQ1742 .P795 2021 (print) | LCC HQ1742 (ebook) | DDC 305.40954--dc23
LC record available at https://lccn.loc.gov/2021002083
LC ebook record available at https://lccn.loc.gov/2021002084

ISBN: 978-0-367-18282-3 (hbk)
ISBN: 978-0-367-18283-0 (pbk)
ISBN: 978-0-429-06050-2 (ebk)

Typeset in Bembo
by MPS Limited, Dehradun

Contents

Acknowledgements

Chapter 1: Poem by John Wipp translated and republished with permission of Ellerströms Publishing House

Chapter 2: Quotation from Art India Magazine Vol. 4, Issue 1 (1999), pp. 64-67: 'The Courage of being Rummana', used with permission from Art India Magazine

A prejudiced time and its women in India

Jhuma Basak

Women in India hold a history of survival against violence and oppression, be it domestic or familial violence to public violation, financial oppression to cultural canonisation and deification. The Indian society has a complex layer of gendered discourse ranging from the caste system to class division, as well as rural and urban demarcation. Over time, one notices an increasing level of 'dogmatic' practices, a definitive regimentation of morality being hauled down by state-authority over civil society in India, which is an equally alarming praxis across the world in today's time. In psychoanalytic understanding, Alexandra Billinghurst called this current 'dogmatic' position of the world as the "paranoid-schizoid times" (*The Paranoid-Schizoid Climate: When Fear & Anxiety Rules*, in the present collection). In other words, an immature ego's splitting off of the all-good-object and all-bad-object (in this context meaning leaders of a society) – thereby creating a paranoid-schizoid atmosphere which the society has poor capacity to contain for this rupture. The recent polarization of socio-political and cultural ideologies in India has created more grounds for authoritative dogmatic doctrines to unfurl on society. This edited book of articles examines this intolerant current time using a psychoanalytic lens with a clinical reading of the Indian society in its expression of religion, motherhood, and intimacy as well as the clinical space itself. The interdisciplinary approach brings forth the reflections of social scientists and mental health activists on India's women and their safety against an increasingly bigoted propagation. The proliferation of a particular notion of 'Indian Culture' may be prompting women to assume 'safer' traditional roles, subsequently eroding the country's history of women's struggle to earn their freedom to rights of choices and opportunities.

Perhaps one way of scaring the woman away from treading on public space and indirectly confining her within 'chastised domestic walls' is by attacking her security and confidence in public space, on public road. And this is what may be noticed in the increasing number of brutal rapes and public violence in the country. One is immediately reminded of the 16 December 2016 rape case of Jyoti Singh Pandey, a 23-year-old physiotherapist, who was beaten up, gang raped, and barbarously tortured by six men in a private bus in South Delhi around 9:30 at night when she was returning home after watching a movie with her boyfriend. This case is referred to as the *Nirbhaya* case (meaning fearless) as *Nirbhaya* struggled for life and became the symbol of resistance to rape for women victims in India. Jyoti Singh Pandey suffered serious injuries to her abdomen, intestines, and genitals due to insertion of blunt objects like iron rods, and died on 29 December after fighting for life for over 10 days. The whole nation rose in civil protests. After decades of being in a dormant state, the student community, the youth – our future of India, roared with a significant awakening across the country. With equal horror came the Kushmandi rape in February 2018 in South Dinajpur, West Bengal, where a mentally challenged tribal woman was gang-raped, "grievously brutalized and left for death under a bridge on the Srimati river by her assailants, whose criminal motives may have included the desire to seize her land as well as her body" as mentioned by Supriya Chaudhuri in *"Marked Unsafe": Women, Violence, and State of Risk* in the present collection of essays. And a little earlier, on the 5 September 2017 the journalist-activist Gauri Lankesh was killed by three men who shot at least seven bullets through her at her home in Bangalore around 8pm. She was honoured the Anna Politkovskaya Award for her work against right-wing Hindu extremism, giving voice to women's rights and opposing caste-based discrimination. Needless to say, all this surreptitiously voiced a covert political play of regimentation and fundamentalism by the ruling authority. And through all these facts the message that perhaps came across in the chronicle of time is a provocation of a sense of 'deranged fear' for women, prompting them to stay confined within an illusion of domestic safety and patriarchal control.

Indian Hindu mythology claims to have 33 crore (over 3 million) deities, which the nation devoured in worshipping all throughout the year in various symbolic forms and in different cultural and geographical contexts. So, it appears that while on one hand the woman can only be worshipped and accepted as a deity, the real flesh-and-blood woman is to be denigrated, and ripped off from all her dignity, identity, and existence. And in this gap between the deity and the denigrated, there perhaps lies the sacrificial 'almost-deity-like' position of the concept of 'mother-India' – the all-giving, all-embracing, all-forgiving, all-encompassing nurturing mother in every family. So, motherhood for the Indian woman is perhaps like an almost deceptive desire to attain closest possible to that deity status in her mortal life. As if her only claim to feminine, human dignity lies in her attaining motherhood. Thus, the notion of completeness for the Indian women is the purity and glory attached to motherhood. Related to this is the significance of marriage for the women in the Indian society. This is perhaps what is reflected in Nilanjana Sanyal's treatment of motherhood (in her chapter entitled, *Revisiting Motherhood: The Current Concepts of Psychoanalysis & that of Current Era*) with its rather traditional implications. While on the other hand lies the adversarial denigrated, fallen, 'whore-mother' claiming her right to motherhood that the so-called 'civilized' society denied her (*The Gendered Proletariat: The Sex Work, Workers' Movement and Agency*, 1917). As if to transgress from her fallen 'whore' state to the 'worship-able' mother state is revoked for the sex worker in society. For her, it is her actively reclaiming entry, both physical and psychological, into regular social, communal space from her marginalised 'ghetto' existence into urban space. In this sense, one wonders if it maybe possible to say that motherhood itself is used as a pawn to gain something else for the woman, and almost a communal collaboration to attain that goal. Consequently, yearning for motherhood is rarely related to the desire of having a child per se but rather a more existential, analytically speaking a more narcissistic fulfilment for the denied existence/worth of a woman. Needless to say, in the early 20th century Freud had elaborated the woman's desire for a child as her narcissistic satisfaction (Freud, 1933), but the socio-cultural emphasis in the Indian context adds to this element of existential significance. It is not a surprise that the 'marriage market' in Indian families and psyche play such a strong semblance.

Paradoxically motherhood inadvertently acts as a 'container' for the same Indian woman as much as perhaps religion promises to. Both provide that physical and emotional space through which the woman stays connected, in an unconscious manner, to their 'semiotic' attachment with the feminine, their pre-oedipal dyadic attachment. The emotional dependence is encouraged, but not necessarily for satisfaction but more to control and hold agency of the woman. Motherhood betroths a child for the woman while religion commits an infantile position for the woman keeping her in affective illusion through rituals in both the institutions. It is quite a dichotomous painful position for the woman. And perhaps the success of the patriarchal construct of this is its surreptitious coercion through socio-cultural beliefs and practices, thereby creating 'living myths' and 'legends' out of women of flesh-n-blood, as Monisha Nayar-Akhtar explains in *The Role of Religious Icons and Mythological Figures in Traumatized Individuals: A Psychoanalytic Perspective*. The woman of 'living myths' attain their 'sainthood' through their sacrificial selves within their family contexts. Perhaps here lies a delicate twist of altruistic qualities being transformed into culturally masochistic traits. Interestingly the state of women in India may often seem to be quite enigmatic. At times her internal resistance to such barbarity is awe-inspiring in reality. So, against a backdrop of such moral, cultural, and physical atrocity there was the resonation of the arousal of the voice of 3 million Indian women in January 2019 who built a 'human wall' over 620 kilometres 'in support of gender equality' protesting against the Sabarimala temple that was closed to women of 'menstruating age' between 10 to 50. And perhaps there lies the hope for a free spirit in the inclusive history of India. The 'state of fear' that the state wants to instill in the woman is countered by the redefinition of their claim over public and domestic spheres.

Increasingly it may be noticed that India is being dissected into binaries – not only in the religious and political sectors but equally divided into binaries of the 'feminine' and the 'masculine.' There is the promotion of a certain notion of 'femininity' along with 'Indian-ness' whereby notions of femininity and masculinity are coloured with overt nationalistic right-wing clout, further enhancing oppositional binaries. In the 1920s, Girendrasekhar Bose, the father of psychoanalysis in India, exemplified India's cultural leaning towards bi-sexuality, derived from his reading of Hindu mythological ancient texts as well as from his clinical references. One wonders whether the post-independence era has witnessed a rigorous unconscious cultural cleansing measure as a re-action to the post-colonial response to 'western imperialistic sanitization' that may have projected a 'purer' sense of 'Indian-ness' – and thus, all allusion of the bisexual leaning in the development of sexuality and gender has been eradicated from reference. There remains the question as to whether this 'sanitized' Indian imago perseveres as the national agenda for today's political predisposition of India. Needless to say, the cultural construct of the Indian woman and her psyche is invariably determined by such a dominant ideology. This engineering of fundamental binaries, the subtle gendered exclusions unfailingly enters into the clinical space for the psychoanalyst, as so poignantly elaborated by Mallika Akbar in her paper, *Peeping Through the Keyhole*. The analyst/therapist is challenged with their fantasies, stimulated in counter-transferential journeys along with their analysands. The self-analytic journey continues for the analyst, and with every analysand it is different. Innovative narrative structures of consciousness are built from an amalgamation of mutual fantasies and the unconscious communion between the analyst and the ana-lysand. Perhaps Indian psychoanalysis needs to re-look at Bose's theoretical delineation on bisexuality precisely at this critical socio–cultural–political juncture of India. It is a time when gender inclusivity is a strong implanta-tion coming from modern India and her liberated, independent women pushing against the popular tide of the fundamentalist right-wing global political climate that is devouring India equally.

Born in this juxtaposition of a politically coloured terrain and culturally hegemonic environment, the modern Indian woman is faced with negotiating conflict in both her 'private' and 'public' spheres. And the growing sexual violence in the public space adds to the fear induced by both the state and civil society in this emotionally disrupted way of being for the woman. However, hope lies in witnessing this transformation in the new progeny of the youthful, dynamic, modern woman who questions and challenges the authoritarian voice both within familial boundaries as well as in the national domain. Perhaps optimism is found in these individuals, or groups of individuals, who hold the ego capacity to both contain and counter the paranoid schizoid position of the family and the state in order to claim familial/societal respect and authentic position, and to nurture pockets of reciprocity through re-parative reflection. This quality of reparation calls for it to be generated and cherished in the patriarchal realm. And women have the potential to sow the seed for this delicate transformation – a different maternal endowment per-haps. It is here that we can find the more complex and deep-rooted surrep-titious reason for the growing public atrocity inflicted on women in recent times. And is that an overt reaction to archaic fear of crass patriarchal abjection/castration? Perhaps the new leaders of today's India are to evolve from this oppressed sector of the women in the country who brave to negotiate the laws and violence of patriarchy poised in their own feminine historicity.

References

Bose, G. S. (1920). *Concept of Repression*. Pub: G. Bose.

Bose, G. S. (1949). The Genesis & Adjustment of the Oedipus Wish, *Samiksa*, 3, 4. Pub: Indian Psychoanalytical Society.

Bose, G. S. (1933). A New Theory of Mental Health, *Indian Journal of Psychology*, 37.

Freud, S. (1933) New Introductory Lectures on Psycho-Analysis & Other Works. Lecture XXXIII, Femininity. S.E XII. London: Hogarth Press, pp. 133–135.

Ghosh, S. (1917). *The Gendered Proletariat: Sex Work, Workers' Movement, and Agency*. Pub: OUP.

Kakar, S. (2008). Maternal Enthrallment: Two Case Histories, *Culture & Psyche*. Pub: OUP.

Nandy, A. (1983). Towards an Alternative Politics of Psychology, *International Social Science Journal*, 35.2: 323–338.

Part I

Introduction to Women's safety in dogmatic times

COWAP Kolkata

Gertraud Schlesinger-Kipp

This chapter brings together two different approaches to the same theme: the meaning of 'women's safety in dogmatic times.'

First Alexandra Billinghurst, a psychoanalyst from a 'safe' country, Sweden, explores what 'dogmatic times' are. She refers to the schizoid-paranoid climate – a psychoanalytic term – which is originally developed (by Melanie Klein) to describe a normal position in the development of a child and a state into which every individual can regress in times of crisis and torment. Everything is black and white, the 'other' does not exist as an individual with their own needs and thoughts, but is fragmented into good and bad. There are no spades of shades between black and white. She then uses this position to describe group dynamics in institutions and also in society. Schizoid-paranoid climates can lead to seeing the other only as enemy, as fragmented and not human and hence can justify wars and atrocities.

Relating to gender and violence Billinghurst explains male violence against women as a breakdown of 'metaphoric thinking' and a regression to the schizoid-paranoid state where no empathy for the pain of the woman is possible. Billinghurst concludes with hopes that democratic societies are more able to retain the 'depressive position,' where care and shelter for the other, and respect, understanding, and reparation reign.

Suprya Chauduri, a female professor of English literature in India offers a different point of view in *Marked Unsafe: Women, Violence and a State of Risk*. This term "marked unsafe" is a creative variation of the Facebook provision "marked safe" when individuals are in disaster zones. 'Being safe actually implies that one is not safe' but alive in a disaster zones. Chauduri describes incidents in India of horrific gang rapes of young girls and women and the reactions of the feminist movement. She questions if there is a specific character of violence against women. Contained in the demand of a "male" right to sex, Chauduri explores the viewpoint in patriarchal societies that sexual pleasure only means male sexual pleasure. She criticizes the traditional Freudian view of the concept of unconscious and its emphasis on sexual desire in human motivation. "The patriarchy encodes and performs a constructed Maleness that performance requires and derives pleasure from the subordinated woman." In that environment 'safety of women' can suggest an abusive term because the woman herself is responsible for her safety, i.e. staying at home, dressing modestly, not going out at night, etc. However the greatest danger is in the woman's own house, and how to dress has not much to do with rape.

Chauduri supports her arguments with different statistics in India, offering the insight that India is the most unsafe country for women as poignantly portrayed by the killing of female babies. She describes the increased number of well-educated women in India enrolled in universities. Yet these universities and workplaces do not prepare women for free living and emancipated life.

Together these two papers open a wide and deep consideration from psychoanalytic and societal perspectives on violence especially in dogmatic times.

1   The paranoid-schizoid climate: When fear and anxiety rules

Alexandra Billinghurst

The following text was a contribution to a conference dealing with threats to women´s safety in society today. Psychoanalysis has been used not only to understand the individual on the couch but to understand groups, organisations, and culture as well. The current trends in society, with political movements calling for the traditional and with views of 'the other' as a threat and enemy, is a situation that causes concern and worry. To see the other as a threat, I'm sad to say, seems to grow in the COVID-19 pandemic. Where nations, rather than trying to unite in the fight against the virus, close up and find ways to blame other nations for the spread. Using psychoanalytic theory to understand the underlying dynamic is one tool we can use to find ways to bring change and to see that there is hope.

On dogma and dogmatic

The meaning of the word *dogma* can be described as a belief or an opinion presented as a fact. A presentation often in an authoritative way and presumably for the individual believed to be true. With other words, believing something is true, without the ability to question and reflect on that which is posited. As a psychoanalyst using psychoanalytic understanding 'dogmatic times' could in my perspective be re-named 'paranoid-schizoid times.'

In order to reflect on what we see happening in the world in general today a short description of Melanie Klein's depressive position and the paranoid-schizoid position is in place.

Melanie Klein (1882–1960), was an Austrian-British psychoanalyst in practice in the UK between 1926–1960 who worked psychoanalytically with small children (rather revolutionary at that time) and developed Sigmund Freud's theories using observations from her work with children. The psychological development of children is often described in phases or stages. Sigmund Freud, for example, described the psycho-sexual development, the oral, anal, phallic, and genital stages. Melanie Klein instead used the term 'positions.' In using position rather than phase she stressed the fact that the psychological development goes back and forth, not in a straight line and furthermore, that either one of us can enter the paranoid-schizoid position at any point in life.

The paranoid–schizoid position

The paranoid–schizoid position is characterized by a split inner world where the outer world and important figures are seen as either all good or all bad. The infant is not able to perceive other people as whole, with their own needs, but rather as functions. For example, when the baby is hungry and the mother feeds him, the baby perceives this as a good, satisfying object. But when hungry, and the mother is not there, the baby perceives (her) this as a 'bad object.' The main anxieties in this position, whether as a baby or later in life, are persecutory with fear of annihilation and of being attacked. This position is also characterised by omnipotence and lacking the ability of reciprocity, of understanding the other's needs. For a person in this state of mind, others are thus part objects, that is, *existing as functions* for the subject. The splitting of the object is in itself not pathological during development but functions as a primitive defense against anxiety and pain and is necessary for a healthy development. It is when an adult lacks more mature defenses that splitting in an individual can be seen as pathological.

The depressive position

In this position it is possible to direct conflicting feelings towards the same object (instead of splitting the object in a good object and a bad object). The main anxieties in the depressive position (looking at a small child) are separation anxiety, fear of losing the object, and then of losing the object's love. In this position, we have the ability to feel guilt and thereby the wish to repair. We have the ability to love the other person for their own sake not for the gratification it gives, whether as a baby or grown-up.

In the paranoid–schizoid position on the other hand, guilty feelings are reversed and felt as attacks from the person the guilty feelings would be directed towards. Rather than feeling the guilt, the other person is given the blame for the situation. A normal teenager will oscillate between those two positions; at one moment being able to take responsibility for his feelings and actions, the next blaming the world around him and especially his parents or siblings.

Let's look at an example from ordinary life of a paranoid–schizoid perception of the world. During an interview with a man, he is asked about his girlfriend and why she is so important to him. He describes her beauty and how his business contacts are impressed with her when he brings her along. Furthermore, he talks about how she will be able to arrange nice dinner parties when he needs to represent. As the interviewer is trying to deepen the picture of her, all she gets is the surface value of the girlfriend, her looks, or her abilities to be of service to him. He is not really able to give a three-dimensional picture of his girlfriend. He is describing love and admiration but there is a lack of description of her as a person in her own right. She is seen more as a status symbol. She is idealized, but that also means that she could at any point be devalued and easily be exchanged for another.

Let me now introduce Wilfred Bion and his thoughts. He has contributed to the understanding of both group and individual phenomena.

Wilfred Bion (1897–1979) was born in India and then went to England to go to college. During the first world war, he served in the Tank Corps in France as a tank captain, an experience he refers to when speaking of containment, which is one of the most important concepts Bion gave us.

Containment

Containment is originally a military term.

A force contains another. Containment presupposes one who is containing and someone/something that is contained. An object, a thought, an idea, a feeling is placed in a containment in such a way that something happens or does not happen with that which is placed.

Containment has to do with meaning. Closely related to the concept of containment is Bion's concept of Reverie. Bion writes that the movement between the paranoid-schizoid position and the depressive position is to be in a state of unconnected, in a field of pieces or fragments. The movement toward depression means that different parts are connected, often as a selected fact. A pattern takes shape. Finding the pattern's meaning is the role of the container-contained function. To put yourself in a state of reverie is to make possible the destruction of context/connection, to not be stuck in focused thoughts, but to let the connection be destructed so that new connections can be found. Within this description lays the idea that being in the depressive position can also mean being stuck in a locked view, of not being able to have a fresh perception.

Reverie

This above description of being in a state of reverie is of the psychoanalyst in reverie. But the state of reverie is mainly referred to as belonging to the mother.

For the baby, being born without the instrument of understanding and memory, every experience could be described as a bombardment of raw sensations in the very beginning of life. From hunger pangs experienced as a painful presence rather than an absence of food, to the supposedly pleasurable feeling of the sun shining through the window, a light breeze on the skin, or sudden sounds around her. As the child has no apparatus for understanding these perceptions yet, it is the role of the mother's (and father's) reverie.

Parents who easily wake up to every little sound of the baby but can sleep through everything else is an example of the function of the parental reverie. A side note here. There is a study (Abraham et al., 2014) of a change in the amygdala in parents of infants. Researchers already knew that the mother's amygdala is changed by hormones during pregnancy, but this study shows that the more the father takes care of the baby the more his amygdala is changed as

well. The study also looked at homosexual parents where one was the biological father, but both fathers tended the baby. Both fathers showed the same
change in the amygdala. This was a little sidetrack, but I find it very interesting
in relation to reverie.

So the parent of the infant has a constant unconscious focus on the babies
state. An example: a mother would suddenly be filled with a conviction and
dread that something was seriously wrong and that her baby was dying.
Having been filled with that emotion she would then calm herself and realize
that her baby is hungry and go to pick her up and nurse her while talking to
her, saying 'You are hungry, come let's sit here, I'll feed you.' This is an
example of both reverie and containment. She had sensed distress in her baby.
The mother experienced the overwhelming scary feeling of being hungry, for
the baby, raw sensations, as a threat that she was dying. An important aspect
here is that she was fully in that feeling and then calmed herself, understanding
that the baby needed to be fed, the raw sensations were with the mother´s help
transformed to something understandable. With her voice and the way she
touched the baby, she transmitted that what the baby is feeling is OK. In this
way lending her transformation function to the baby. With the recurring of
this over time, the baby slowly builds her own transformation function. I want
to point out that it is not just the calming voice and touch that is important
here, but also that the baby in turn has sensed the mother´s distress, her anxiety, and then the transformation from fear to calm. This transformation gives
the baby a sense that what is scary can be survived, i.e., contained.

As we grow up, we all have an established transformation function, where
raw experiences can be transformed and given meaning. This function can
break down, as in trauma or intense distress. But it is also the case that you can
have an established function but with certain areas where the transformation is
not working. If a child has a parent for whom certain feelings are very anxiety
provoking or not "supposed to exist" the child will not get help in understanding those feelings in herself. In that case you wind up with a person who,
when certain feelings arise, get into a state of anxiety.

The containing function is vital for us as individuals but also for a group, an
organisation, or society. The containing is also intertwined between these different levels. In a group with a weak leadership the lack of containment can affect
the individual's containment in a negative way and vice versa, an individual's
ability to contain can transform the ability for the group to contain. To perceive
and give meaning to what goes on inside or in the surrounding environment.

Coming back to the positions above, Bion thus developed the idea of the
positions further. According to him, not only is it *possible* to continue oscil-
lating between the positions but it is actually *necessary* and something to
strive for.

According to both Melanie Klein and Wilfred Bion, in the paranoid-
schizoid position we have a very set view. There is no space for shades between black and white. In this position people are either idealized or feared
and despised. Some people remain in this position, such as in the case of

personality disorders where the individual for some reason has not developed more mature defenses. But, as stated earlier, we can all be thrown into this position when, for some reason, our inner world and our sense of security is threatened.

Group and organisational dynamics

Humans are group beings. Belonging and being accepted by our group is important to the individual, and signs of being pushed out of a group leads to reactions of shame and fear.

Bion, and later the Tavistock group, have shown how powerful the group as its own unit, is. In a group setting you can find yourself doing and saying things that you would not normally do.

Bion speaks of The Work Group and the Basic Assumption Groups.

The Work Group is what it sounds like, a group that is able to work with its task towards a goal.

The Basic Assumption Groups are defending against anxieties and in the Assumption state the group is stuck.

There are three kinds of Basic Assumptions:

Dependency: The group becomes passive and looks for rescue from confusion by a strong leader.

Pairing: The group turns to a couple who are seen as an idealized hope for producing a solution for the group's problems.

Fight/flight: In this assumption, the group either fights to preserve the group at all costs or flees from its task. Here, too, the group looks for a strong leader inside or outside the group and in fight mode the atmosphere can be aggressive and hostile.

My experience with groups and organisations has shown me how a group dynamic can 'sit in the walls' of for example a unit at a hospital. Although all the members of the original group have been exchanged, the same group patterns find itself come to life in the group, over and over again.

In the world of psychoanalysis, as vice president of IPA, I have seen examples of how organisational problems and splits in a society can be traced back to conflicts in the beginning of that organization's life, many decades ago. It lives on in an unconscious way and then erupts into a new conflict. Seemingly a conflict over a new subject with strong feelings on both sides. Both parties feel convinced they are the holders of 'the truth.'

If one starts examining the history of the society you might then find a conflict between the founding leaders that was never properly solved. In gaining knowledge and understanding of this historic fact the groups might be able to loosen their beliefs that only they carry the truth and instead develop an atmosphere with a high celling where there is space for more than one position on say, a theoretical matter. That is, just as uncovering unconscious conflicts in an individual can lead to a positive change intra-psychically, the same can be true for groups and organisations.

Leadership in organisation and society is crucial and can either contain its members or be destructive and create splits. That is, create a paranoid–schizoid atmosphere.

One way a leader can do this is by choosing favorites. Or by failing to see the group dynamics in a conflict and focusing on individuals instead. An individual is seen as the cause of a particular problem rather than seeing the group or organization as a whole. You know you are in such an organization if you start feeling paranoid, fearing attacks from others.

Violence, and women as a threat to men

In understanding violence against women, we can of course both look at the individual and the group/societal perspective.

In clinical work in outpatient psychiatric clinics and in private practice, I have had experiences of women who have found themselves in or that are trying to leave abusive/controlling relationships. More common is that these women do not themselves see that they are in an abusive relationship but where they instead search psychiatric or psychotherapeutic help for depression or anxiety. For them, being abused either verbally and/or physically is 'normality' and it is only through a safe atmosphere in therapy, where the therapists question the normality of abuse, that the woman can start to question the abuse herself.

There is usually a very specific pattern in these relationships. They start with the man courting the woman in a very romantic and attentive way. The woman often describes this as feeling loved in a way she has never experienced before. He picks her up from school or work and wants to know everything from her day. When he starts to show jealousy, this is seen as a proof of his strong love for her. From the outside it might be obvious that it is a controlling behavior, but for the woman it has become her daily reality. This turns into a switching between praising and idealizing her to calling her names and blaming her for being a slut when she speaks to male coworkers for example. After being abusive he might be very apologetic, bringing her flowers and promising he will never hurt her again.

From my position as therapist or psychoanalyst, I only have the woman's perspective and as I have not met these men in person I cannot actually diagnose them, but they seem to range from men who are more narcissistic/have a narcissistic personality disorder to men that seem to be able to have well-functioning relationships but oscillate between the positions in how he perceives his important figures. That is, at times seem to actually see his partner's needs but then start experiencing the world and his woman from a paranoid–schizoid position.

I want to share with you here an interesting article I found when searching to understand violence in intimate relationships, "Metaphor and violent act" by Campbell and Enckell. Campbell and Enckell wanted, with their study, to understand the violent act from the perpetrator's perspective. Regarding metaphors they write: "…a metaphor consists of a combination of words uncombinable according to ordinary logic."

They then go on to describing how the foundation for the psychic function of the individual starts before there is language, where the perception of the world goes through the body sense and the relationship to the early caregiver. Furthermore, how the early experiences lay in the unconscious as wishes that have no representation. In psychotherapy and psychoanalysis in general, metaphors are created that bridge the gap between preverbal and the patient's current inner narrative. Through the metaphor the wish or experience gets representation. But the authors also "… believe that the metaphor model can be seen as a model of general psychic work, defined as the work of representational interconnecting" and go on to say that for some individuals the metaphors in the cases they have studied, can turn concrete when the anxiety gets too high so that which was a symbol feels like a concrete reality.

They ask "Why do some individuals defend against primitive anxieties about survival by defense mechanisms that rely upon symbolization and metaphor while others resort to violence? We believe the answer lies in a failure of metaphor to contain anxiety. With the breakdown of metaphorisation, the individual regresses to non-verbal modes of defense."

They illustrate several cases where the metaphors used in the subjects turn 'concrete' when a situation in the relationship with the woman is seen as a threat to his psychic integrity. "These configurations of their internal states were not sensed as ordinary metaphors. Mr Giles and Karl did not feel *like* being trapped, and Mr Wilson did not feel *like* being left in the dark: Mr Giles and Karl felt they *were* engulfed and Mr Wilson thought he *was* in a life-endangering, isolating blackness. It is worth noting that all three men were, in fact, articulate, and used metaphors in an appropriate way during ordinary conversation. However, metaphors failed to function in an ordinary way when Mr Giles and Mr Wilson felt themselves to be in certain forms of danger.

The use of metaphors in psychic work could also be described with the words of Bion. That is, the transformative work described earlier. That which the parent does for the infant through her containment and that the infant slowly starts to be able to do herself.

The authors describe, I think very illustratively and clear, the dynamics behind how a man is able to turn physically violent towards a woman. The women in these cases being felt as threats to the man's integrity. I believe that on a group level, women can also be perceived as a threat to men.

Both in times of societal development where the traditional ways are questioned, especially for men in lower economic strata who find themselves having less and less power. For them, women become a symbol of losing their male identity.

But also in dogmatic times.

Living in a paranoid-schizoid climate

The world has seen incredible changes just in the last few decades. With the Internet we are suddenly connected to the rest of the world and news can be spread with lightning speed. It used to be we were given news from around the world in a form digested by journalists in our own local or national media.

With the Internet we are suddenly given live images at the push of a button. I think that in itself is a strain on our containing functions as individuals. Our ability to feel empathy is strained. We want to be able to help, to comfort, but with so much pain in so many places we lack the power to help. That is, without ability to find meaning.

If we perceive a threat there is a risk that we turn to the known and familiar by enhancing the traditional. And that we put up 'walls' making those on the other side of the wall enemies, or people who deserve what is happening to them.

In our globalized world where globalisation has been seen by many as something positive, what we see happening is a trend of groups of people and some politicians and governments wanting to strengthen the nations more, turning nationalistic. From a psychological perspective I do think it can be understood as a wish to find a more manageable cohesion. A clearly defined 'home.'; The problem is that it becomes a 'we' and 'them' mindset and a paranoid-schizoid climate where all that are unknown are enemies rather than people to get to know. While those within the nation and its leaders are idealised, fear of the other reigns.

Historically the world has been in a paranoid-schizoid climate before, leading up to the World Wars for example.

Today we see populist and extremist political parties growing and entering parliament in 'unexpected' places all over the world.

In extremism and populism, the world is described as black and white, the all good and all bad. Groups of people are described as foreign, enemies, a threat to 'us,' and 'our' traditional values. In Sweden, the extremist party is calling for Swedish traditions and naming examples. Examples that if examined can be shown to have been brought into Sweden a 100 years ago by people who, with the same description by the extremist party, would be called "foreigners" and a threat. When pointing to this fact in a dialogue with representatives of this party such facts are completely dismissed or ignored. That is, in line with the definition of dogmatic, "believing something is true, without the ability to question and reflect on that which is posited."

Or to quote Shapiro and Carr where they describe group function and phenomena, where a group turns against another group or an individual: "Through shared unconscious assumptions, groups manifest this phenomenon by developing rigid, stereotyped views of individual members or of other groups that are unchanged <u>by additional information.</u>" (Shapiro and Carr, 2012). Additional information being coined 'fake news' for example.

What I can discern about the current situation in India, through what reaches me through Swedish media, is that nationalism seems to be on the rise at the same time as there are great advances economically. I also hear about a greater division between faiths. I can imagine that women, for groups of men, and individual men, may be seen as a personal threat to the known and familiar. So that the attack can be compared to what Campbell and Enckell describe, of the metaphor becoming concrete.

In the current COVID-19 pandemic, we are faced with a threat both as individuals and as societies. It is in such a situation that mature leadership is crucial. If the leadership can maintain the ability to contain, the society and individuals can be protected against falling in to the paranoid-schizoid view of the world. With such an intense threat these first reactions are understandable. Sadly this global crisis has shown how fragile the international collaborations are. In many places we can observe how the pandemic threat has spiraled the paranoid-schizoid reactions into even worse threats to the safety of the people in many societies. But we can also observe the opposite movement to the depressive position, in, for example, how researchers start sharing their findings freely with other researchers in order to more quickly find medicine that can potentially save lives and in order to develop vaccines.

Gender roles and power

The violence in intimate relationships described previously can also be seen as a return to a more traditional gender role pattern between the woman and the man. To him, the "'reedom' of 'his' woman's work becomes a threat to his own identity as the protector of the woman/family.

In speaking about women's safety, at this point in recent history, it is hard not to also mention the #Metoo movement.

What I think has been eye opening for so many women, is that what they felt was normal, something to live with, or something that they thought was just happening to them, that they felt ashamed of, turned out to be a general pattern of men seemingly thinking they have the right to women's bodies. What we see here again is an example of when a pattern is suddenly coming to light. Of women standing up and questioning. In a newfound connection/community that forms a new group, finding the strength to question authority and dogmatic beliefs.

Another recent example is the school shootings in Florida. One of so many. But where suddenly a group of teenagers question the authority and clearly point to how the right to carry guns, something so highly held, is actually what made the shooting possible. The right to carry guns is, by many, seen as a metaphor for freedom in America. And in the school shootings it becomes the concrete metaphor, described by Campbell and Enckell but on a societal level and in this case in the narrative following the shooting.

The extremist populist wave can be seen as an oscillation to the paranoid-schizoid position on a societal level and the #Metoo movement and the movement by young people against the NRA as an oscillation to the depressive position.

A pattern was perceived, and in the discovery new groups formed, and strength was found to stand up to it.

A transformation happening before our eyes that I do think gives hope.

Democracy is the foundation for most societies. Democracy does not mean that the best way forward is always found. Democracy cannot be taken for granted, it has to be protected, kept alive, and nurtured. A democratic society can still find itself in a paranoid-schizoid position with authoritative leadership. But individuals, and groups of individuals can through their containing function notice/capture this fact and make the oscillation towards the depressive position. The depressive position where respect and understanding for the individual and the perceived foreigner is held high. Where reciprocity and reparation reigns. Where it is possible to question authority and to reflect.

I would like to end with a poem. It is by a Swedish artist and poet, John Wipp (translated by me). I chose to include it here because I think it captures that each and every one carries the ability and risk of falling into the fear of the other, into hate and defenses that obscures empathy and care of the other. Only by understanding that, of understanding the mechanism in division, reflecting and taking responsibility for our own darkness within us, can we as individuals, groups, and societies, withstand and develop in dark and dogmatic times.

> Let the darkness
> within me, for me
> be visible
> Like the bottom of the pond
> as I with my hand
> screen the light from above
> so as not the surface
> shall mirror
> the depth of the sky
> The depth
> which the light
> reflection conceal
> lives. Transforms
> under shiny membranes
> which I have to see through

References

Abraham, E. et al (2014). Father's brain is sensitive to childcare experiences, *Proc Natl Acad Sci U S A*. 2014 Jul 8; 111(27): 9792–9797.

Bion, W.R. (1959). Attacks on Linking. *Int. J. Psycho-Anal.*, 40:308–315.

Bion, W.R. (1961). *Experiences in Groups and Other Papers*. London: Tavistock.

Bion, W.R. (1962). *Learning from Experience*. London: Tavistock.

Bion, W.R. (1963). *Elements of Psycho-Analysis*. London: Heinemann.

Bion, W.R. (1970). *Attention and Interpretation: A Scientific Approach to Insight in Psycho-Analysis and Groups*. London: Tavistock.

Campbell, D. Enckell, H. (2005). Metaphor and the violent act. *Int. J. Psycho-Anal.*, 86(3):801–823.

Klein, M. (1975). Envy and Gratitude and Other Works 1946–1963: Edited By: M. Masud R. Khan. *The International Psycho-Analytical Library*, 104:1–346. London: The Hogarth Press and the Institute of Psycho-Analysis.

Shapiro, E.R. Carr, A.W. (2012). An Introduction to Tavistock-Style Group Relations Conference Learning. *Organ. Soc. Dyn.*, 12(1):70–80.

2 "Marked unsafe": Women, violence, and the state of risk

Supriya Chaudhuri

There is today a global epidemic of violence: wars, genocides, terrorist attacks, mass rapes, abductions, sexual assaults, domestic abuse, hate speech, and casual mayhem in public places. The idea of safety is itself in question: What does it mean to be safe? Is safety the absence of harm, or the suspension of threat? For women, safety is a problematic notion since it implies a state of risk, the condition in which most women find themselves every moment of their lives. Adapting a phrase from social media, we could say they are *marked unsafe*. Since the Facebook provision of marking oneself safe is only offered in disaster zones, being safe actually implies that one is not safe. Already in 2013, the World Health Organisation had reported that physical and sexual violence affected over a third of women globally (WHO, 2013: 2–5). This reflected a long-standing crisis, intensified rather than resolved with every passing year. Recent campaigns such as *#MeToo* and its corollaries have highlighted the pervasiveness of the problem without indicating a solution. There is little retroactive justice for women, or improvement of conditions on the ground. Given the enormous psycho-social cost of this daily violence, endemic to societies the world over, we need to ask some hard questions.

No more Kushmandi?

Let me begin with an incident close to home, in my own state of West Bengal in India. On Saturday, 3 March 2018, a small protest rally in south Kolkata under the banner 'Kushmandi Ar Noy [No more Kushmandi],' led by two activist women, Swati Chakraborty and Monisha Mukherjee, marched to demand justice for the victim of a horrific gang-rape carried out at Dehabandh Hatpara village in Kushmandi, South Dinajpur (17 February 2018). The victim was an Adivasi woman, 21 years old, who was abducted, raped, brutalized and left for dead under a bridge on the Srimati river by her assailants. This crime, fully as grave as the notorious 'Nirbhaya' rape and murder in Delhi (December 2012), did not bring thousands of protestors out on the streets of the national capital. The chief minister of West Bengal intervened to ensure treatment for the survivor at Malda Medical College Hospital. Two men were arrested. On Friday 23 February, an angry assembly of Adivasi people, armed with traditional weapons and drums, arrived at the village of one of the perpetrators and burned down four houses belonging to his family. This was a reminder of similar scenes of mass violence after the rapes of four Adivasi women, two of them minors, in July 2017 at Raiganj in North Dinajpur. In November of that year, after the rape and murder of a 12-year-old Adivasi girl, a villagers' forum gave the police three days to arrest the culprits, threatening a complete shutdown of the area if they failed to do so. But not much was done, despite the rage and despair of the Adivasis. In fact, questions of poverty, exploitation, caste, and land ownership are as much at issue here as sexual violence, since sexual violence is itself only an expression of power relations in society, as every woman knows.

What then was the point of the slogan 'No more Kushmandi,' under which a couple of hundred women and men rallied in the city of Kolkata? Such occasions are liable to be co-opted by the interests of political parties, and given the sad regularity of crimes, abuses, and violence in everyday existence, how could the call to stop rape, to ensure women's safety, be anything more than a temporary rallying cry expressing obstinate hope, not practical foresight? The idea that civil society could be *united* on this platform ignores the misogyny and oppression within society that make such crimes possible. In India, outpourings of anger and grief followed vicious assaults like the Bantala incident in 1990, the Nirbhaya case in 2012, the Kamduni case in 2013, the Kathua abduction, rape and murder of a child in 2018 – events that caught the public eye and produced public catharsis. But as Jacqueline Rose noted recently: "while attention to violence against women may be sparked by anger and a desire for redress, it might also be feeding vicariously off the forms of perversion that fuel the violence in the first place" (Rose, 2018: 3). Feeding off – and also feeding? Many recent cases of assault have a frighteningly similar character, as though the perpetrators are learning from each other.

Whose safety?

Victims of violence are not exclusively women: they include many vulnerable categories, like children, poor and marginalized people, Dalits (members of oppressed castes in India), persons of colour, transgenders, addicts, vagrants, the mentally ill, victims of terrorism or of 'collateral damage' in conflict zones. Safety should mean safety for everyone, and there is no sharp distinction between victims and abusers, since abusers in one situation may have been abused in others (as bullying teaches us). The *#MeToo* campaign is still un-covering horrific stories of long-term abuse, of young boys as well as girls: in the recent documentary film *Leaving Neverland* (2019), two men speak of childhood abuse by the singer Michael Jackson. Worldwide allegations of sexual abuse in the Catholic Church range from the conviction of Cardinal George Pell and the defrocking of Theodore McCarrick, to charges of rape levelled in 2018 by a senior nun in Kerala, India, against Bishop Franco Mulakkal. Women's safety, like the feminist movement itself, is related to other social issues of oppression, injustice, and violence. But is there a specific character to violence against women that might justify its separate treatment? Historically, the feminist movement was distinguished from other struggles by its effort to address extremely widespread – if not universal – structural imbalances in human societies, inequalities naturalized to the extent that only radical psychic and discursive readjustments could make them visible. At the same time, the human rights argument had to acknowledge our own complicities within other structures of injustice and oppression: class, race, caste, not gender alone. Feminists were not always attentive to this, just as class struggles habitually disregarded persisting gender inequalities. In what has been called a postfeminist age, advances in the struggle for basic rights seems to make traditional feminisms obsolescent, yet gender issues under patriarchy are revealed in their full complexity, affecting men and LGBTIQ individuals as well as women. What then would be the philosophical justification for singling out the issue of women's safety?

Bodily rights

My argument here is that feminist struggles still have urgency and relevance: the climate of risk inhabited by women has specific, identifiable features. Sexual violence is only one of the forms of violence experienced by women, but here as elsewhere, distinct pathologies are involved. In a recent essay, the philosopher Amia Srinivasan asked, 'Does anyone have the right to sex?', focusing on homicidal violence by self-proclaimed 'incels' (involuntary celibates) like Elliot Rodger, who killed six people in Santa Barbara, California, in 2014, and Nikolas Cruz, who killed 17 at Marjory Stoneman Douglas High School in Parkland, Florida, in 2018. 'Incels' are persons unable to satisfy their sexual needs because they cannot attract partners. Subsequent to the publication of Srinivasan's article, Alek Minassian drove his car into a Toronto sidewalk in April 2018, killing 10 people (eight women), having posted on Facebook that 'The Incel Rebellion has already begun! All hail the Supreme Gentleman Elliot Rodger!' The majority of self-proclaimed incels are male, and the 40,000-strong incel 'support group' on the online platform Reddit (shut down for inciting hate in November 2017) was largely populated by white men, many of whom advocated rape and nurtured fantasies of violence.

On the global scale the dreamt-of 'incel rebellion' is a relatively minor sociopathic aberration. But it allowed Srinivasan to ask hard questions about rights. Men who demand sex as a right (though women could be involuntary celibates, they do not seem to raise such a demand or enforce it) and hate women for denying it to them, claim another person's body, cancelling out her autonomy. Srinivasan states, axiomatically, that "no one is under an obligation to have sex with anyone else" (Srinivasan, 2018: 8). Fantasies of sexual entitlement are produced by patriarchal systems treating women (and gay men) as usable commodities, like slaves in the market of sexual labour. (Marital rape is still not a crime in India.) Radical feminist critique had condemned the violence implicit in *all* sexual relations under patriarchy. Catharine Mackinnon wrote:

> the organized expropriation of the sexuality of some for the use of others defines the sex, woman. Heterosexuality is its structure, gender and family its congealed forms, sex roles its qualities generalized to social persona, reproduction a consequence, and control its issue. (1982: 516)

Reflecting on sexual violence *as sex*, Mackinnon explained that gender inequality, which is organised and structural, allows men to experience assault as sexual pleasure, and women to associate pleasure with subordination or femininity. Her campaign, with Andrea Dworkin, against pornography as the mode in which sexual abuse is made an object of cultural consumption, and her views on how sexuality is codified as sexual terror, offered a bleak picture of gender relations in society, and left no space, so her critics argued, for male or female desire. Was sexual pleasure only men's pleasure, and therefore abusive? Radical feminism was divided on this issue, since it appeared to taint *all* sexual pleasure, and placed an impossible burden of guilt and self-deception upon women in heterosexual re-lationships. Srinivasan notes the counterview of the cultural critic Ellen Willis, vital to the 'pro-sex' versus 'anti-sex' debates within radical feminism in the 1980s and 1990s. Analyzing these struggles, Willis argued that 'radical feminists as a group were dogmatically hostile to Freud and psychoanalysis, and psychoanalytic thought—especially its concept of the unconscious and its emphasis on the role of sexual desire in human motivation—had almost no impact on radical feminist theory' (Willis, 2012: 135). She argued that to assign all the responsibility for structural inequality and abuse to men was 'a false logic,' because it assumed that the impulse to dominate was a *male* characteristic, rather than 'a universal human characteristic that women share, even if they have mostly lacked the opportunity to exercise it. "It's a logic that excludes women from history not only practically but ontologically, and it leads to an unrealistic view of women as a more or less undifferentiated underclass with no real stake in the power struggles of class, race, and so on that go on among groups of men" (Willis, 2012: 123).

Willis is here trying to address the intersectionality of gender inequality with other kinds of inequality in society, an historical problem for radical feminists, given their "lack of a class analysis or strategy that transcended the women's movement" (Willis, 2012: xvii). Recent, highly publicised campaigns around sexual abuse, harassment, and the lack of safety for women in public spaces have only rarely embraced issues of class, race, caste, or economic opportunity. Willis is right in rejecting the notion of an *essential*, abusive 'maleness' that is prone to violence: but in so far as patriarchy encodes and performs a constructed male-ness, that performance requires, and derives pleasure from, the subordination of women. Women also have a stake – how could they not? – in 'the power struggles of class, race, and so on' (see Willis above), but their situatedness, at the intersection of domination and pleasure, constitutes their special state of risk, and exposes them to *violence as pleasure* – that is, sexual violence.

Weaponising rape, imagining the 'birangona'

At the other end of the scale from the 'epidemic' of everyday violence is the use of rape as a weapon of war. In 2008, the United Nations Security Council Resolution No. 1820 declared that "rape and other forms of sexual violence can constitute war crimes, crimes against humanity, or a constitutive act with respect to genocide" (UNSC, 2018 (1820): 4). Rape had already been classed as a war crime by the International Criminal Tribunal for Rwanda in 1998. The UN Resolution acknowledged this afresh, but international condemnation did not prevent an increase in rapes, say in the Democratic Republic of the Congo, or by Boko Haram in Nigeria. In India's neighbour Bangladesh, between 100,000 and 200,000 women were raped during the liberation war of 1971, chiefly by the Pakistani army and its local collaborators. The Indian army has also been accused of weaponising rape, notoriously in the villages of Kunan and Poshpora in Kupwara, Kashmir, in February 1991, and in the killing of the activist Thangjam Manorama in July 2004, near Imphal in Manipur.

In an essay in *Daedalus* (1996), the anthropologist Veena Das noted that 'unprecedented collective violence' was inscribed into the birth of the Indian nation, one of its signatures being 'the large-scale abduction and rape of women' during Partition. To speak of such suffering involves the Emersonian gesture, as she calls it, of approaching the world through mourning for it. The pain of abused and violated bodies renders spectral and illusory the image of the heroic or nurturing woman on whom nationalist ideology was projected (Das, 1966: 67–68). This is acknowledged in the 'feminist turn' in Partition historiography, exemplified in Urvashi Butalia's *The Other Side of Silence* (2000), or the two volumes of Jasodhara Bagchi and Subhoranjan Dasgupta's *The Trauma and the Triumph* (2003-09). Feminist studies of the hidden struggles of women in workers' and peasants' movements (the work of Panjabi, Rege, Pawar, Omvedt, the Stree Shakti Sangathana, and so on) have recorded women's resistance as well as their suffering. Das's essay inspired Nalini Malani's powerful five-screen video installation, 'Mother India: Transactions in the Construction of Pain,' 2005, which linked the phantasm of 'Mother India' to the suffering of women even in the later cataclysmic violence of Gujarat in 2002. Das wrote the foreword to Nayanika Mookherjee's book *The Spectral Wound* (2015), a study of sexual violence, public memory, and state intervention after the Bangladesh liberation war of 1971. Mookherjee examines the figure of the *birangona,* or warrior woman, constructed by the government to valorise survivors of wartime sexual violence and provide them social and material compensation. The first self-acknowledged *birangona*, the Bangladeshi sculptor Ferdousi Priyabhashini, died in March 2018. In an interview, Mukherjee commented on 'the sociality of violence':

> Instead of thinking of stigma, shame and scorn as given categories, we
> need to understand when and why these categories are raised. Here I

would argue stigma is often raised as an arsenal for local, everyday politics, to keep someone who is already maybe weak as weak, or dominated as dominated, or unequal as unequal. So there is a political economy of stigma, honour and shame. (Mookherjee, 2016: n. p.)

The introduction to Mookherjee's book reproduces Naibuddin Ahmed's celebrated photograph (1971) of a woman who had been raped by the Pakistani army (Mookherjee, 2016: xvii). But Mookherjee is aware of the pitfalls of an ethnography of violence, especially the unreliable trope of giving voice to the subaltern or breaking the silence around crimes against women. The *birangona* figure is itself a kind of public performance: in the aftermath of the Liberation War, artists, actors, photographers, writers, activists, created a serial enactment though which national honour was 'restored' through visual representations, theatre, oral history projects, and exhibitions. Mining this extensive textual and visual record, the book ends with the protests at Dhaka's Shahbagh square in 2013 and the execution of Abdul Kader Mollah on 12 December. It recognises the ubiquity of sexual violence, and the discomforts and uneasiness that attend its public acknowledgement as a war crime. Rape was only one of the offences for which many wartime 'collaborators' accused of crimes against the people were tried before the war crimes tribunal instituted by the Awami League in 2009. The young protesters who took part in the Shahbagh movement knew that the history of 1971 contained secrets, memories, betrayals, and contradictions that might never be resolved, bringing out "the war between oneself and one's image in the mirror" (Mookherjee 275, citing Ghosh, 1988, 204).

Despite these measures, to this day only around 40 *birangonas* – out of a lakh or more – have publicly acknowledged their experiences of rape during 1971, though these histories are known and many such women were supported by their families. The public memory of the *birangona* in Bangladesh is paradoxically bound up with public secrecy: the two 'complement each other,' and their intertwining offers an alternative to the nationalist narrative, 'highlighting its ambiguities and tensions with everyday lives and imaginaries' (Mookherjee, 2016: 14–15). Moreover, as the artist Naeem Mohaiemen wrote, 'progressive and feminist projects can also have their own forms of silencing,' and 'even more disturbing than these quiet blind spots are the way feminist struggles can also be appropriated by the war on terror project' (Mohaiemen, 2017: n.p.).

Women's safety in 'dogmatic times'

Mohaiemen raises a number of complex issues. Let us pause for a moment to consider what women's safety means, especially 'in dogmatic times.' Just as there is a 'political economy' of honour, stigma, and shame, so too is there a political and social economy of safety. To start with the assumption that women are not safe is to buy into the neo-conservative argument that we are always-already in a state of exception, a condition of extreme risk where measures to ensure safety will necessitate the curtailing of women's freedom. Historically, feminism has met this argument head-on, taking risks in the dangerous struggle for freedom, and courting anger, abuse, and oppression in order to access public spaces. It has demanded a just and equitable social order where risks are equally shared. The problem is that the social order we inhabit is so skewed by patriarchy that risk – indeed, extreme danger – is already written into the context within which women must operate. As a result, those risks can be leveraged to support damaging recommendations by fundamentalist religious leaders, or political functionaries, that women should dress 'modestly,' remain within their homes, not go out at night, not use mobile phones, and so on. The idea of safety becomes, effectively, an *abusive term*, an instrument of social tyranny: particularly when the responsibility for being safe devolves upon the victim, rather than the abuser. Yet women are most in danger at home; abuse largely takes place within the family and from persons known to the victim, and dress and social habits have very little to do with assault (UNODC, 2018: 13). Globally, one woman in three is likely to suffer domestic violence. India's belated *Protection of Women from Domestic Violence Act,* 2005, affords some protection, though it still does not criminalise marital rape. In 2006, the junior minister for women and child development, Renuka Chowdhury, stated that 70% of Indian women suffer domestic abuse (Chowdhury & Jha, 2006). The Thomson Reuters Foundation cited government data in March 2017 to the effect that nearly 20,000 (19,223) Indian women and children were trafficked in 2016, an increase of nearly 25% from 2015; the highest number of victims being recorded in West Bengal (TRF, 2017).

In 2018, the controversial Thomson Reuters Foundation survey (TRF, 2018) found India the most unsafe country in the world for women, ahead of Afghanistan, Syria, Somalia, Saudi Arabia, Pakistan, and the Democratic Republic of the Congo. India also leads in human trafficking, 'cultural traditions' that militate against women, and sexual violence (USA, ranked tenth overall, is third in the last category). The poll was contested by India, with the National Commission for Women dismissing it outright and pointing out that countries where women are kidnapped and used as sex slaves by militant groups, as in Nigeria, Iraq, or Syria, did better in a survey based not on data or statistics, but the 'perception' of 548 'experts.' Six different indices were used: healthcare, discrimination, cultural tradition, sexual and non-sexual violence, and human trafficking. Sanjay Kumar, director of the Centre for the Study of Developing Societies (CSDS, Delhi), questioned the poll's lack of transparency: 'How were these people chosen? What is the gender divide? Where are they from?' (BBC News, 2018, 28 June). The perception draws on increased publicity and sensitisation for cases of rape and sexual violence. But the statistics on women are too grim to allow complacency.

In a recent essay, Mary John, former director of the Centre for Women's Development Studies, New Delhi, reflects on the fact that: 'violence has become a kind of touchstone for the recognition of an issue as a 'women's issue'. "The presence of coercive force—in a whole range of acts from rape to sexual harassment—appears to crystallise feminist issues, renders them recognisable as such, and even enables them to acquire resonance within a larger, otherwise unsympathetic public" (John, 2019: 3). The link that John makes here between women's rights and physical safety is important, given her own role as co-chair of the committee that framed the University Grants Commission *Saksham* report (2013), on women's safety and gender sensitisation on campuses. The report had noted how the Delhi rape (December 2012), the Justice Verma Commission's *Bill of Rights for Women* (January 2013) and the *Sexual Harassment at Workplace (Prevention, Prohibition and Redressal) Act*, 2013, had countered the 'invisibiliza- tion' of sexual violence in society (*Saksham* 13), but it emphasised that gender sensitisation was virtually absent on most campuses (35). Students believed that universities "should help women transition from the protected atmosphere of the home into a real life situation where she had to be independent" (37). But five years on, after the *#MeToo* movement of 2017 that touched both campuses and workplaces, John sees a link between sexual violence and the fact that while women are now present in much larger numbers in higher education, their presence in the waged workforce is appallingly low (only 15% according to NSSO figures: John, 2019: 8). This lack of economic independence is key, John feels, to persistent social inequality and oppression.

"Thinking with (not against) the touchstone of violence," John suggests that the institutional, even feudal culture of universities had left women un- prepared to cope with, even to name, the kinds of exploitation and harassment that accompanied supposedly progressive attitudes, revealed through *#MeToo* and Raya Sarkar's Facebook list of prominent men in Indian academia anonymously accused of sexual harassment (John, 2019: 9–10). Thus the 2014 'Hokkolorob' agitation at Jadavpur University had turned on an incident of sexual assault, and the 'Pinjra Tod' and *#Take Back the Night* movements demanded safe and free movement for women (Chaudhuri, 2019). In closing, John cites Nancy Fraser's *Fortunes of Feminism* (2012) to ask whether neo- liberalism in India, taking the road of 'jobless growth,' had hugely increased the vulnerability of women, whether in elite workplaces or at the lower end of the spectrum (11). Incidents of sexual violence or exploitation all too often provoke expressions of communal hatred, misogyny, and class division, since women's safety in India is rarely separate from questions of society and politics. Not only are women blamed for being assaulted, but a pervasive rape culture answers assault with the threat of 'revenge rapes.'

A state of risk

This data suggests the logical conclusion that the present social order, with its entrenched political and economic structures, is itself a state of risk, and that in patriarchy, women are marked unsafe. Feminists have long been pressing for this conclusion, arguing that the socialisation of women in patriarchal cultures normalizes violence, and effects lasting damage, both physical and mental, on women – and also on men. The 2013 WHO report cited above notes the enormous toll, in terms of "mental disorders, somatoform disorders or chronic illness, as well as other physical conditions," taken by this endemic, everyday violence. Its manifestations – stress, neuroses, trauma – "encompass physical, sexual and reproductive, and mental health, with potentially large impacts on levels of women's morbidity and mortality" (2013: 7). Fundamentally, this was what the *#MeToo* and *#TimesUp* campaigns were about: rather than seek justice for long-past acts of sexual harassment, they sought to bear public witness to the extent of psychic damage caused, over long periods of time, to women, and also to gay and trans individuals, by a toxic male culture of exploitation and sexual entitlement, which is what patriarchy is. In a perceptive essay, Trina Nileena Banerjee builds on older feminist arguments to suggest that in a hetero-patriarchal world, pleasure and danger are tied together at the root: female sexual desire, even a state of being at home in one's body, 'invites' assault, while male sexual desire asserts proprietorship and control (Banerjee, 2017).

In *Civilization and its Discontents* (1930), written when he was already ill, Freud offered the 'astonishing' contention that 'what we call our civilization is responsible for our misery.' Freud describes a human society where, as he put it, quoting Plautus, *homo homini lupus*, man is a wolf to man: "[their] neighbour is for them not only a potential helper or sexual object, but also someone who tempts them to satisfy their aggressiveness on him, to exploit his capacity for work without compensation, to use him sexually without his consent, to seize his possessions, to humiliate him, to cause him pain, to torture and to kill him" (Freud, 1985: 302). Civilisation partially inhibits these desires, producing unhappiness and disappointment. Freud concludes that "If civilization imposes such great sacrifices not only on man's sexuality but on his aggressivity, we can understand better why it is hard for him to be happy in that civilisation" (1985: 306). While Freud uses male pronouns throughout, he is, not infrequently, referring to the human race as a whole, and in that respect 'aggressivity' has to be understood as a quality common to all humans. Yet the tone of Freud's lament tends to make the burden of civilisation and its suffering almost exclusively male, rendering phantasmal the cost (elsewhere identified as hysteria or melancholia) that this scheme of things must exact from women.

The pain of others

But does the problem of violence actually *originate* in male 'aggressivity,' object-love, and anxiety occasioned by the fear of loss? In 1938, the year after her nephew Julian Bell was killed in Spain, and faced with the threat of another European war, Virginia Woolf wrote a three-part essay called *Three Guineas*. She asserted a direct link between masculinity and violence, asking for a retreat from war and a rejection of all the institutions through which patriarchy reproduces its habits of aggression and tyranny. She called upon her readers to bear witness to suffering and pain, to discipline their eyes so that she and they might look "at the same picture ... the same dead bodies, the same ruined houses" (1966: 11). In that seeing, "we are not passive spectators doomed to unresisting obedience but by our thoughts and actions can ourselves change that figure. A common interest unites us; it is one world, one life. How essential it is that we should realize that unity the dead bodies, the ruined houses prove" (Woolf, 1966: 129–30). That unity, suddenly glimpsed in the ruins of the houses and the bodies, is an important corrective to the absolute binary of masculine violence and feminine resistance that Woolf has been building up. It is a corrective, too, to the idea that we can locate – in effect, contain – violence by ascribing it to a single origin, ignoring its tendency to contaminate social structures and blur psychic motives. In *Regarding the Pain of Others* (2003), and even more in a later essay called 'Regarding the Torture of Others' written after the circulation of the Abu Ghraib photographs, Susan Sontag notes the erotic charge, a lust of viewing, that affects the viewer as it appears to have affected the photographer on the scene. If patriarchal culture produces a profound social imbalance, that imbalance is also liable to seep into the psychic lives of individuals, making the roles of victim and abuser, griever and grieved, interchangeable.

Figuring resistance

How then can resistance be figured – resistance to violence that is also a critique of its traditional structures? Women writers and artists in India have offered a sustained critique both of everyday and of 'exceptional' violence, in such a way as to bring the two together in a single frame. Literary re-presentations are relatively better known, but it is worth reflecting on such 'public art' projects such as the wall stencil of a young girl (with a number, and the word 'missing') put up in multiple locations all over Kolkata by the artist Leena Kejriwal, to remind us of India's skewed sex ratio, and all the missing girls, murdered at birth, for whom the question of safety does not even arise. For my final example, however, I would like to return to the complex re-lationship between dogma, safety, risk, and violence, as represented in an artwork that becomes a text of resistance.

Just before her death in 1999, the Indian artist Rummana Hussain appeared in a spoken performance called *Is it what you think?* where she read out a questionnaire designed to test the identity and conformity of the female subject to religious and social norms. The text was excerpted in full in an essay by the art critic Geeta Kapur, who describes Rumanna's performance showing 'self-reflexivity developing in the besieged subject (who is the object) of world-wide pity, curiosity and scorn' (Kapur, 1999: 65). The questions restate social anxieties, even as Rumanna, identifying as 'a Muslim woman,' purports through 'a recited text to parry religious taboos, hegemonic Islam, forced privacy, undesired intrusion' (1999: 66):

Where does she belong? Is she behind a veil? Have you defined her? Does she go into her shell? Have you pushed her? What does the press say? Do social conditions alter her behavior? (1999: 67)

As Kapur makes clear in her brilliant reading, the artist is here deliberately masking her own liberal or secular identity, the work she does with the radical art collective, SAHMAT, by showing what it is to be 'a Muslim woman artist in a climate of a de-secularised India, [and] this is a reiteration of the secular in a paradoxical way' (1999: 67). The questions open up the distance between the woman's own selfhood and the social imperative that seeks, incessantly, to question, define, and categorise her, to establish whether she conforms to familial or religious expectations, whether she has been secretly radicalised, whether she obeys her father, does chores, and so on:

Do you think that she has radical views? Do you think she can articulate them? Do you think her voice has been stifled? Is that fact or fiction? Have you defined her? Is she the other? (1999: 67)

Through a body that had already experienced pain and loss, Rummana Hussain made performance a means of questioning safety, gender, religion and culture in an India torn apart by communal violence. Uncannily prescient, her interrogation anticipates how the physical body of a young Muslim activist woman, Safoora Zargar, arrested and denied bail for her alleged role in fomenting the north Delhi Hindu-Muslim riots of February 2020, has now become a site of patriarchal and state control (*Scroll*, 2020). By challenging our understanding of the social place of women, Hossain offers a mode of cognitive resistance to systems of controlling violence.

References

Banerjee, Trina Nileena. (2017). "Carceral" or "Sex-positive"? *Seminar Magazine*. At: http://www.india-seminar.com/2017/691/691_trina_nileena_banerjee.htm Accessed May5, 2019.
BBC News. (2018). (28 June). Is India Really the Most Dangerous Country for Women? Report on Thomson Reuters Foundation survey. At: https://www.bbc.com/news/world-asia-india-42436817 Accessed March 14, 2019.
Chaudhuri, Supriya. (2019). On making noise: *Hokkolorob* and its place in Indian student movements. *Postcolonial Studies* 22:1: 44–58. DOI: 10.1080/13688790.2019.1568168.
Chowdhury, Renuka and Nilanjana Bhaduri Jha. (2006). Exclusive interview: Renuka Chowdhury. *The Economic Times*. November 7: At: https://economictimes.indiatimes.com/news/politics-and-nation/exclusive-interview-renuka-chowdhury/articleshow/350533.cms?from=mdr Accessed March 14, 2019.
Das, Veena. (1996). Language and Body: Transactions in the Construction of Pain, *Daedalus* 125:1 (*Social Suffering*), 67–91.
Fraser, Nancy. (2012). *Fortunes of Feminism: From State-Managed Capitalism to Neoliberal Crisis*. London: Verso Press.

Freud, Sigmund. (1985). *Civilization and its Discontents.* In: *Civilization, Society and Religion.* The Pelican Freud Library, vol. 12. Harmondsworth: Penguin Books.

Ghosh, Amitav. (1988). *The Shadow Lines.* New Delhi: Ravi Dayal.

John, Mary E. (2019). Sexual violence 2012–2018 and #MeToo: a touchstone for the present. *The India Forum.* At: https://www.theindiaforum.in/article/sexual-violence-2012-2018-and-metoo Accessed on May 5, 2019.

Kapur, Geeta. (1999). The Courage of being Rummana *ART India Magazine.* 4(1): 64–67. (I am grateful to Geeta Kapur and the editor of *ART India Magazine* for permission to quote from this article).

Mackinnon, Catharine. (1982). 'Feminism, Marxism, Method, and the State: An Agenda for Theory'. *Signs,* 7(3): 515–544.

Mookherjee, Nayanika. (2016). *The Spectral Wound: Sexual Violence, Public Memories, and the Bangladesh War of 1971.* New Delhi: Zubaan Academic.

Mohaiemen, Naeem. (2017). Time of the Writing, the Hour of Reading. In: Brandel, Andrew and Meyers, Todd. 'Book Forum', *Somatosphere.* February 11, 2017, at: http://somatosphere.net/2017/02/book-forum-nayanika-mookherjee-the-spectral-wound.html Accessed March 14, 2019.

Mookherjee, Nayanika and Preetha, Sushmita S. (2017). 'Ethical challenges of documenting Birangonas'. *The Daily Star.* September 18. At: https://www.thedailystar.net/in-focus/ethical-challenges-documenting-birangonas-1463638 Accessed March 14, 2019.

Rose, Jacqueline. (2018). I am a knife. *London Review of Books,* 40(4). 22 February: 3–11.

Saksham. (2013). *Measures for Ensuring the Safety of Women and Programmes of Gender Sensitisation on Campuses.* New Delhi: University Grants Commission.

Scroll. (2020). https://scroll.in/latest/963851/delhi-violence-pregnant-jamia-student-safoora-zargar-denied-bail-for-third-time Accessed June 7, 2020.

Sontag, Susan. (2007). Regarding the Torture of Others. In: *At the Same Time: Essays* and *Speeches.* New York: Farar, Straus and Giroux, 128–142.

Srinivasan, Amia. (2018). Does anyone have the right to sex? *London Review of Books,* 40(6). 22 March: 5–10.

TRF. [Thomson Reuters Foundation]. (2017). Nita Bhalla. 'Almost 20,000 women and children trafficked in India in 2016'. At: https://www.reuters.com/article/us-india-trafficking/almost-20000-women-and-children-trafficked-in-india-in-2016-idUSKBN16G29G Accessed May 5, 2019.

TRF. [Thomson Reuters Foundation]. (2018). *The World's Most Dangerous Countries for Women.* Accessed on March 14, 2019 at https://poll2018.trust.or.

UNODC. [United Nations Office on Drugs and Crime]. (2018). *Global Report on Homicide. Gender-related killing of women and girls.* At: https://www.unodc.org/documents/data-and-analysis/GSH2018/GSH18_Gender-related_killing_of_women_and_girls.pdf. Accessed on May 5, 2019.

UNSC. [United Nations Security Council]. (2018). Resolution 1820. At: http://undocs.org/en/S/RES/1820(2008) Accessed on March 14, 2019.

WHO [World Health Organization]. (2013). *Global and regional estimates of violence against women: prevalence and health effects of intimate partner violence and non-partner sexual violence.* Geneva: WHO Press.

Willis, Ellen. (2012). *No More Nice Girls: Countercultural Essays.* Minneapolis: University of Minnesota Press.

Woolf, Virginia. (1966). *Three Guineas.* Orlando: Harcourt.

Part II

Revisiting motherhood in contemporary times introduction and commentary

Paula L. Ellman

This section on *Revisiting motherhood in contemporary times* offers a paper on by Prof. (Dr.) Nilanjana Sanyal's chapter, *Revisiting Motherhood: The concepts of psychoanlaysis and that of the curent era*. This paper offers a review of the perspectives on traditional ideas of motherhood and a consideration of contemporary perspectives. She begins with an optimistic view of the healthy, productive, nurturing aspects of motherhood, and discusses the transgenerational impact of the maternal imago with consideration of the maternal representations occurring in pregnancy. The author provides a summary of Stern's work on the motherhood constellation, addressing the themes that emerge in development with the transition to motherhood.

Dr. Sanyal keeps close to traditional descriptions of the maternal role vis a vis the child and the husband and specifies the differentiation in role as lactating versus non-lactating organisms. I believe that many current writers might take umbrage with Dr. Sanyal's emphasis on a classical strictly traditional consideration of maternal familial role as we now have many permutations of acceptable successful ways of raising children where role differentiation may be more diffuse or ambiguous, or along different role differentiations, between women and men, men and men, or women and women. Also, with her consideration of current trends where women can both have careers and at the same time have children and be a mother, Dr. Sanyal suggests that it is in being a mother that is the primary most important expression of womanhood. Nonetheless Dr. Sanyal emphasises that the more current working-mother defies this expectation and offers her ideas on the influence of early archetypal origins of motherhood on today's version of motherhood. In her description of the power of the mother for the infant, the source of nurturance and love, the author recognises that this power can also engender fear, offering an important preliminary suggestion about the ambivalence that the infant can hold for the mother. There is the "good mother" and the bad witch mother. The power of the mother can make for envy, rage, and even at times the wish to destroy, as we witness globally in the form of misogyny. The author speaks to the Hindi legend of Durga, the Protectress of the World and creative feminine force and likewise in many cultures there are myths of the powerful mother figure.

The author examines dimensions of the "mother" in object relations theory by reviewing Bowlby, Klein, Winnicott, and Chodorow, yet pays less attention to the introjected mother, and more to the real mother. Throughout, she places her emphasis on the mother-child bond, its importance in securing attachment, and in allowing for differentiation and separation. The author finally does bring her recognition of a new maternity where previous limits to reproduction no longer hold and possibilities for motherhood have expanded.

This paper brings a lively enriching discussion to the realm of motherhood in contemporary times.

3   Revisiting motherhood: The concepts of psychoanalysis and that of the current era

Nilanjana Sanyal

Within the existential bonding of human relationships, the mother-child dyad seems to be the most cherishable one in physical, developmental, and emotional tunes. Of the myriad glittering facets of womanhood, it is generally said that the experience of motherhood completes the cycle of sensing and feeling the woman-contents explicitly. In a healthy context, mothers are outstanding personalities in one's life. They are the source of our existence, they are the best protectors, crusaders against the predators in life, they are 'all embracing' in terms of warmth – the providers of unconditional love to develop 'trust' in external life. This, being the background scenario, day has come to revisit the concept of 'motherhood,' its various patterns in today's world to draw the true implications of such a figure in our life.

To the infant, mother appears as a "global, inchoate, all-embracing presence," as unbounded and amorphous, as the "monolithic representative of nature" (Dinnerstein, 1976:93, 95). As Benjamin (198:77) points out, "the view of mother as object resounds throughout our culture." Mothers and women remain for us closer to object than to subject, closer to nature than to culture. Mother in the prevailing patriarchal culture is one who takes care of our sustenance and all of our wants and needs endlessly (Gray, 1982:102–5). Mother thus seems to be the best resource-asset in a child's life. The childhood idea of mother paints her as an omnipotent protector, the all-pervading, all-embracing wrapper on us. With growing age, with gradual exposure to reality, the solid bases of object-relations re-paints the mother images in reality tones but the traces of earliest cozy emotions with mother stays with us.

Motherhood has different vicissitudes which can be understood through different colours of love and other emotions in relation to the child. A healthy relational bond with a child is expected to be the outcome of a positive experiential bond of the mother with her own mother. In fact, early childhood experiences are found to be the bases for our specific personality orientation that helps us to develop specific perspectives to life. In a healthy relational context between the mother and the child, the tune is like, "What I had from my mother, I would give you more." However, the ideal of motherhood also unconsciously contributes to the wish for a child on her part, a fantasized opportunity to play out the role of mother and child in an ambivalent idealized form desired in the woman's childhood. In this fantasy, the woman wants to be the mother she wanted to have (Alizade, 2006). The necessity is felt to explore the intricacies of maternal representations during pregnancy in the present juncture in order to fathom the in-depth emotional impact of mothers in women's lives.

Maternal representations in pregnancy

a.   *"The motherhood mystique"*

Motherhood involves enormous transformations in a woman's life. It may seem to be the most natural thing in the world, a biological privilege accorded only to women. Biological theories assume that women are programmed to care for children; socialisation theories assume that women are more nurturing because of early learning. But it is just as likely that a nurturing personality is created by being put into a nurturing role as an adult. The process of mothering is a kind of doing gender that produces womanly persons (McMahon, 1995). Motherhood involves the desire to experience pregnancy and birth, to participate in the growth of another human being, to please a husband or partner, to strengthen a relationship, to prove oneself as an adult, to be needed and loved, and to pass on a family name or one's genes or one's values.

Some radical and cultural feminists, on the other hand, have pointed out that motherhood is a woman-centred model of how people can be connected and caring (McMahon, 1995). Western society has strong beliefs about motherhood. The ideology of motherhood revolves around the motherhood mystique having inherent different myths as follows:

1.   The ultimate fulfillment of a woman relates to motherhood.
2.   Women are instinctively apt at caregiving of their children. Good mothers enjoy this kind of work; a woman who does not is maladjusted or poorly organised.
3.   A mother needs to have infinite patience and sacrificing bent of mind, otherwise, she ceases to be an adequate mother.
4.   Intense, full-time devotion of a woman to mothering is best for her children. Women who work are inferior mothers (Hays, 1996; Hoffnung, 1989; Johnston-Robledo, 2000; Oakley, 1974). This myth persists because it has important functions for men (Hays, 1996; Lorber, 1993b).

Women are encouraged to sacrifice other parts of their lives for motherhood, which then creates economic dependence on men and is used to justify women's lower status and pay. During a desired pregnancy, both positive conscious and unconscious fantasies, having their origin in childhood, become activated. This consequently brings about alterations in the woman's object-libidinal and narcissistic equilibrium. A marked shift towards libidinal concentration on the self takes place. The dual and expanding self-representation of the self consisting of the mother and the developing foetus is underlined by a specific type of narcissism. It brings about a feeling for the pregnant woman that the growing baby is an integral part of her own self-system. This puts forth a symbiotic relationship of the woman with her future child where she engages in fantasy to mould her wishes and ego-ideal. Thus the infant-to-be becomes enmeshed intimately with the mother's self. This gets disrupted when the foetus moves within the mother's body, with gradual development, finally resulting in birth (Rothbaum, Rosen, Ujiie, & Uchida, 2002).

Stern's motherhood constellation

Stern (1995) holds that a woman, when pregnant, poses into a new and unique psychic organization which he calls the *"motherhood constellation."* It concerns three different but related preoccupations. Having a child brings about eminent changes in a woman's life. The discourses, being referred to as *"motherhood trilogy,"* may be outlined as follows (Stern, 1995):

* *the mother's experience of 'mothering' with her own mother;*
* *with herself, especially herself-as-mother, and*
* *with her baby.*

Stern (1995) also believes that the following related themes emerge:

* *a life-growth theme*, which means that the mother is apt to look after the life and sustenance of the baby
* *a primary relatedness theme*, which refers to the emotional relatedness of the baby with his/her mother in a reciprocal manner
* *a supporting matrix theme*, which means that the mother knows how to create and permit the necessary support systems to fulfill these functions and
* *an identity reorganization theme*, which refers to her ability to transform her self-identity to permit and facilitate these functions.

Each theme tends to influence the mother's feelings, actions, interpretations, interpersonal relations, and their adaptive behaviour in relation to the baby. In fact, the idea of being in motherhood reorients the mother-to-be and gets her ready for re-adaptive behaviour in life to suit the new role she has acquired. These four themes and their related tasks are named the *"motherhood constellation"* by Stern (1995). He argues that the motherhood constellation that emerges, may be permanent, transient, or permanently revocable.

The woman in relation to her motherhood

A woman's biological destiny, as mother appears to be, is determined by culture-specific notions. It is often debated that mothers serve the role of 'socializers' of children and thereby achieve their main social position. Her suitability for socialisation springs from her physiological condition, her ability to lactate, and occasionally relative inability to undertake strenuous workloads. Levi-Strauss Shapiro 1956 opines that womanhood is associated with child birth and caretaking of the baby and normally fatherhood is associated with the role of social protector and provider for the family. The concept seems to be an age-old one. The situation can be conceived as a teleological evolution, like a mother generally wishes to care for her child that embellishes a trail in her mother, with which women have been generously endowed. Since caring for and maintaining a child to adulthood is the maternal job and decisional condition, motherhood can be conceived as a platter of women empowerment. However, the cultural allocation of roles in bringing up children and the limits of its variability does not seem to impede the bio-emotional urge of the mother to take care of the child. Automatically, this fact can be accounted in the context of women empowerment.

The nuclear family revolves around generational hierarchy. In typically Parsonium idiom, this lies in the division of organisms into lactating and non-lactating classes; the male plays the instrumental role in relation to the wife-mother. The mother plays an instrumental and expressive role in her 'mirroring role' with the infant which, in turn, fosters development. She becomes the source of approval and disapproval, love and care in the pre-oedipal stage of the child. However, after this, the father or male substitute takes over (Ahuja, 1999; Seymour, 1999).

The familial objective of procreation as well as the role of pursuing one's occupation successfully appears to be two important activities that an adult engages in the modern scientific society. The function of the family as such reflects the primarily expressive function of the women within itself. However, such a person playing an integrated-adaptive-expressive role is a utopian concept resulting in a built-in inhibition of the woman's work outside the home. This leads to non-empowered concept of women/mother in general. The current working-mother scenario defies it thoroughly.

The current scientific notion of childhood enables in reasserting women's quintessential maternal function to the fullest extent. The emphasis of familial ideology has shifted away from a cult of the biological ordeal of maturity to a celebration of mother-care as a social and cultural act. For the mother, breast-feeding is often complemented with creation. This ensures a sense of fulfill-ment in relation to the mother-child bond (Bowlby, 1958). It enables a woman to express her total self with tender care, feelings, and nurturant at-titudes. The root of personal adequacy of the child gets embedded there.

Thus, psychological theorising seems to take account of women's sub-jectivity and agency and of the inter-relatedness of mothering with other culturally informed relationships and values to accommodate existing cultural variation and complexity in the roles of women as mothers and in relationships of mothers to children (Barlow, 2004). At this juncture, the need is felt to understand the origin of motherhood in terms of archetypal frame to deduce its implications in modern motherhood concepts. This is attempted to be sketched in the following section.

Motherhood having its archetypal origin

The notion of motherhood may be related to the 'mother–maiden' archetype. The prominence of the Great Mother in the psychic and cultural life of humanity is noteworthy in this respect. In fact, Jung and his adherents have found in the image of the Mother Goddess a fruitful field for the application of myth to human consciousness, the development of the feminine psyche, and the role of woman in the family (Makowski, 1985). The mother archetype plays a key role in the unconscious domain of every individual in accordance to Jungian theoretical notion. The indelible impression of the 'mother-experience' in the formative layers of mind is universally common. As birth-giver, as nurturer, as the infant's means of sustaining life, the mother exerts an incalculable effect upon her offspring's conscious and unconscious development. The mother appears to be a 'pillar' of security, trust, and warmth for the child. Simultaneously, however, the same mother, because of inconsistency on her part, can be a source of fear to the child as he/she is completely dependent on her for the sustenance as well as maintenance.

From a Jungian perspective, these polarities evidence themselves in the dual aspects of the Mother archetype, namely, the Good Mother and the Terrible Mother (Neumann, 1955). On the one hand, while the Good Mother is unconditionally accepting, 'containing' and caring in nature, on the other hand, the Terrible Mother, is an equally familiar character in the traditional tales of many cultures and is represented in the witch, the wicked stepmother, and the Gorgon. According to Thompson (1981), maiden, matron, and old crone are the three images of the Goddess which are related to the archetypal relationships of the female in relation to the male. The Hindu and specifically the Bengali sub-culture has its predominant belief in the Primal Spirit who covers the universe. People bow down to their feet worshiped by the world – the Protectress of the world – Durga (June, 2004). Durga is regarded as an embodiment of creative feminine force or Shakti, believed to be the fierce form of Lord Shiva'a's wife, Parvati. She is regarded as the Universe's Mother because of her inherent personality features. The Goddess Durga is associated with fertility and threat (being a goddess of vegetation called Shakambhari as the folk dimension of the myth goes), a warier dimension, being the militant Goddess to kill the devil, a Sanskitic side, and a moral aspect. She is the goddess of courage and strength who conquers the demon of lust, a defender of purity, and is a young bride who visits her parents for three days each autumn. She is also a loving mother to her children who call upon her (Bandyopadhyay, 2017). Durga is also regarded as Jagaddhatri, who holds and preserves the universe and thus serves the mother's role. The Great Mother takes many forms in world mythology. She is known as Magna Mater in Rome and associated with the great fertility goddess, Cybele. She is regarded as the savior of the universe from evil forces and destruction.

Campbell and Muses (1991) described the Great Mother in her many different forms as Gaia or Mother Creatrix. She is also referred to as Nammu in the Fertile Crescent and by other names in different places. In essence, she represents the essential unity of mankind and life per se to engage in a sort of vicious cycle (Campbell & Muses, 1991:4–5).

Similarly, the image of Madonna and child is etched in world's cultural consciousness. We equate mothers with Goddesses. Yet the authentic liberation of women is missing from our socio-cultural layers. A transformation is needed to conceive women with equal potentialities and power in terms of appraising motherhood as the source of sustenance in our life (Balint, 1985).

Thus, *mother* is a central figure in the infant's socio-emotional life and *mothering* provides the canvas of experiential medium for the infant. The mother-child relationship, according to Freud (1924), is the first relationship and other relationships are developed in relation to it. Important and widely shared cultural values about social relationships and relatedness are communicated, learned, and acquired in the template of mother-child interactions. In addition, unconscious phantasies are often evoked in mothers by babies themselves that determine the emotive quality of their interaction with each other (Raphael-Leff, 1989).

It is to be noted that in psychoanalytic theory, two major re-workings of Freudian theory have been influential in recasting the role of the mother, namely, Lacanian and object relations theories. The present discourse will attempt to provide a comparative analysis of different theories of mothering along object-relations perspective.

Notion of 'mothering' along different theoretical dimensions of object-relations

Mother-child interactions appear to determine the nature of subject-object relations. Hence, mothers play an important role in installing healthy object relations of their children. Freud opined that the originary union with the mother is conceptualised as the source of peace, trust, security, and bliss. When children realise that their mother is separate and not under their control, their sense of total security and bliss is destroyed. This is extremely painful for the child for which defense mechanisms are often adopted to repress the feelings into the unconscious. Such wounds become the motivation for subsequent symbolic activity in the world (Bowlby, 1969; Erikson, 1950; Freud, 1924; Lacan, 1964).

• *Bowlby's perspective of child's tie to the mother*

In this context, Bowlby (1958) suggests that different positive aspects of the child's tie with his mother may be outlined as:

(1) The child has *a number of physiological needs or secondary drives* which must be met, particularly for food and warmth, but no social needs. With time, the baby learns that the mother is the source of gratification of his/her needs;

(2) There is in infants an *in-built need to relate themselves to the human breast*, to suck it and to possess it orally. This is referred to as the notion of *Primary Object Sucking*.

(3) The inherent need of infants to be in close proximity to the mother-figure and to cling to the person is referred as *Primary Object Clinging*.

(4) Infants have a craving to return to the womb as they often do not feel comfortable as they used to in the pre-natal stage. This is called *Primary Return-to-Womb Craving*.

Thus, Bowlby is of the opinion that attachment behaviour has different independent instinctual responses as elements.

• *Kleinian approach and other associated perspectives on mothering*

Psychoanalytic theorising about mothering has been revised in the form of object-relations theory as developed by Klein (1975a, 1975 b), Winnicott (1965), and others. Such theories focus on "pre-oedipal" mother–child attachment during which the child is presumed to internalise his/her caretaker's attributes, responses, and attitudes as aspects of self. The mother remains 'emotionally sensitive' to the different needs of the child, their successive changes in demand patterns, and in helping them to grow as independent ones having sufficient autonomy. The base point seems to be gratified intimate relational bond at the outset. They often portray "the mother" in essentiated form, and in derived form as an object in the fantasies of infants and young children. For Klein (1975a, 1975b), the mother is most prominent as a symbolic figure in the internal life of her child. According to him, the baby discovers that mother is a whole being, outside the baby's omnipotent control. In Winnicott's (1965) formulation, the mother, is naturalised as intuitively *"good enough."* He identifies the needs for an adequately supportive environment, *"the facilitating environment,"* and makes intriguing suggestions about the relationships among self-awareness, fantasy, play, and culture. Melanie Klein, Margaret Ribble, Therese Benedek, and Rene Spitz each have suggested the presence of a primary social bond between the mother and the child.

• *Notion of 'emotional symbiosis'*

Benedek (1952) advocated the concept of 'emotional symbiosis' to describe the notion of emotional sensitivity and reciprocity between the infant and the mother figure. This runs parallel to Winnicott's (1967) concept of 'mirroring.'

• *Psychosocial perspectives of mothering*

Erikson (1950) has emphasised on the concept of basic trust, which has its origins in orality as he comments, 'The oral stages, then, form in the infant the springs of the basic sense of trust' (p. 75). Spitz (1957) opines that anaclitic attachment of the infant develops on grounds of his/her dependence on the mothering individual which appears to play an important role in survival, in turn.

Fairbairn (1941, 1943) invokes the theory of Primary Return-to-Womb Craving. He emphasises on mother-dependence in the form of orality like other object-relations theorists. His belief that 'infantile dependence is equivalent to oral dependence' (1943, p. 47) prompts him to infer that the initial year of life paves the ground for personality development of the child.

In most societies, being Feminine and Mother are combined to form a single self-representation of "Woman." Motherhood is thus a state of being. It encompasses inherent myths, stereotypes, and beliefs regarding 'ideal mother' concept which get transmitted down across generations.

- ### *Winnicott's infant-centric perspective of mothering*

Of the classical psychoanalysts, Winnicott (1956) in particular binds the mother to her child in her pursuit of a secure attachment resulting in a so-called "primary maternal occupation" (Winnicott, 1956). Winnicott is of the opinion that physical holding of the foetus in the womb calls forth identification of the mother with the infant making her emotionally-sensitive to the baby later. Rossi (1977) argues at this juncture that women's maternal instinct has been genetically programmed as a result of past adaptive needs.

Winnicott's focus, like Klein's, is on the mother-child bond (Klein, 1937, 1946). He regarded the first relationship as reciprocal between the mother and child. The child knows no boundaries between itself and other, the "me" and "not-me" and is exclusively focussed on the helping mother/breast (Winnicott, 1956). Initially, the infant seems unable to discriminate between the mother and the breast and perceives them to be equivalent. This is followed by gradual individuation on the part of the infant. This leads to the steady development of the ego of the child. The child does not have any concept of object permanence during the initial period for which the mother ceases to exist when he/she does not see her. The mother re-enters the child's world when she returns and only then exists again to tend to its needs and care for it.

According to Winnicott, it is through recognition from its mother that the child comes to experience its own existence. The "good-enough" mother creates a "facilitating environment" in which she enables the child to gently discover itself and its boundaries through gradual exploration (Winnicott, 1960a, 1958). This "third area" lies between the infant's boundaries and its mother. The infant gradually learns to tolerate separation from the mother by means of symbolism and play-activities to earn his/her own identity. Winnicott (1971) identifies the need for an adequately supportive environment, "the facilitating environment," and makes intriguing suggestions about the relationships among self-awareness, fantasy, play, and culture. The potential space of the infant, that is developed, is used to explore inner boundaries and relations and to understand its relation to the external world (Fountain, 2000).

Gradually, the infant achieves the ability to explore its inner world by developing the capacity to be alone in the presence of the mother (Winnicott, 1967). Entering a state of "un-integrated being" (Winnicott, 1967), the infant is protected by its mother from impingement from the outside world. The mother's presence is important to the infant's inner world which comes to identify its boundaries and internal relationships. With development, the potential space becomes a place where individuals can learn to mourn lost objects, re-assimilate their attachment, and emerge to re-invest in new objects. The child develops his/her sense of identity gradually which is maintained and modified throughout one's life-span.

Chodorow's cultural perspective of mothering

Chodorow (1999) opined that the role of mothering has an inherent cultural bearing as it enables in determining different gender identities of individuals. Women tend to learn a large part of mothering through identification from their own mothers. This tends to instill a sense of 'womenhood' in them, being culturally ingrained in nature. This seems to bring forth resonating relational and affective context among mothers in accordance to Chodorow. As such, motherhood is culturally determined and not solely a zoological fact.

The facades of motherhood having its in-built flavor have changed a lot in the current century. Revisiting motherhood ideations need a probe into that too. The following section carries the portrayal.

Motherhood in the current century

Motherhood was often described during the early 20th century as the result of healthy developmental trajectory by classical psychoanalysts. Others who differed from this paradigm were considered to be adorned by "masculinity" complex. There have been dramatic changes in the societal context as well as a consequence of which the "right to choose" appears to be the prime label to indicate healthy female development. In the context, the feminist school of thought came into the surface. It states that *desire for self-actualisation* appears to determine one's choice for motherhood or opt out for other avenues. With birth control pills on women's side, biology is no longer a destiny (Alizade, 2006). Instead, one needs to take into consideration women's subjectivity and agency and of the inter-relatedness of mothering with other culturally in-formed relationships and values to accommodate existing cultural variation and complexity in the roles of mothers and in relationships of mothers to children to have a holistic account of the construct of motherhood.

Infertile women, women partnered with infertile men, single heterosexual and lesbian women, and lesbian couples now enjoy the opportunity to have their own children by dint of different rapidly evolving reproductive techniques.

Such individuals are typically driven by strong maternal desire, who have transcended rather than accepted the destiny of their own biology by becoming biological mothers. Hence, such means of assisted reproduction technology are expected to bring forth tremendous changes in the object–relational matrix.

The psychoanalytic understandings of sex, gender, and parenthood have been ripped apart. A sexual union between a man and woman is no longer the prerequisite for procreation. Instead, modern reproductive technologies have brought forth an external third party into the reproductive process. It may take the form of a man/woman who donates his/her sperm/egg, or even a woman who offers her womb as the gestational space for somebody else by being a surrogate parent.

As such, the new maternity challenges the discourses on existing psycho-analytic work on gender, reproduction, and motherhood. It, in turn, paves the way for maternal desire being divorced from sexuality along with a re-framing of the primal scene and associated issues. Foster mothers, single mothers de-void of biological birth, step-mothers, mothers who adopt children for varied reasons and the like appear to be some who seem prominent among those posing for their 'new maternity.' Babies hence can be now born of libidinal *maternal* (or paternal) desire, divorced completely from sexual union. Yet at the same time, the sexualised images that spring from the acts of assisted re-productive technology may be especially poignant for mothers who use donor insemination (Diamond, Kezur, Meyers, Scharf, & Wienshel, 1999). The nature of object–relations for such mothers poses to be a challenge which the current century is expected to witness. Children being conceived of non-sexual union through varied means of assisted reproductive technology are still in their developmental folds of the relational matrix which needs to be probed through the psychoanalytic lens.

Conclusive comments

I feel that 'unconditional giving' is the chief hallmark of motherhood that may cross the territories of sexual union. The notion of 'motherhood' thereby seems to be accompanied by the need toward self-actualisation and to attain the role of a 'complete' human being as far as affective, cognitive, and conative repertoires of mental frame are concerned. This ultimate meta-need of human beings seems to underlie the quest of seeking one's own identity in the frame of motherhood in the long run.

References

Ahuja, R. (1999). *Indian social system.* New Delhi: Rawat Publications.

Alizade, A.M. (Ed.). (2006). Motherhood in the twenty-first century. *Psychoanalysis and Women Series.* London: International Psychoanalytical Association, Karnac.

Balint, M. (1985). *Osnovna greška. Terapijski aspekti regresije* [The basic fault. Therapeutic aspects of regression]. Zagreb: Naprijed.

Bandyopadhyay, S. (2017). A case study of Durgapuja festival of the Bengali Hindus. *Anthropology Open Journal*, 2, 1:15–21.

Barlow, K. (2004). Critiquing the "Good Enough" Mother: A Perspective Based on the Murik of Papua New Guinea. *Ethos*, 32, 4:514–537.

Benedek, T. (1952). Personality development. In F. Alexander and H. Ross (Eds.), *Dynamic Psychiatry*. Chicago: University of Chicago Press. pp. 63–113.

Benjamin, J. (1988). *The bonds of love: Psychoanalysis, feminism and the problem of domination.* New York: Pantheon Books.

Bowlby, J. (1958). The nature of the child's tie to his mother. *International Journal of Psychoanalysis*, 39:350–373.

Bowlby, J. (1969). *Attachment and Loss*. London: Hogarth Press.

Campbell J., & Muses, C. (Eds.). (1991). *In all her names: Explorations of the feminine in divinity*. New York, NY. HarperSan Francisco.

Chodorow, N. (1999). The Power of Feelings: Personal Meaning in Psychoanalysis. *Gender and Culture*. New Haven, CT: Yale University Press.

Diamond, R. Kezur, D., Meyers, M., Scharf, C.N., & Wienshel, M. (1999). *Couple therapy for infertility*. New York: Guiford Press.

Dinnerstein, D. (1976). *The mermaid and the minotaur: Sexual arrangements and human malaise*. New York: Harper and Row.

Erikson, E.H. (1950). *Childhood and Society*. New York: W. W. Norton.

Fairbairn, W.R.D. (1941). A revised psychopathology of the psychoses and psycho-neuroses. *Int. J. Psycho-Anal, 22*. Reprinted in *Psycho-Analytic Studies of the Personality*. (London: Tavistock, 1952).

Fairbairn, W.R.D. (1943). The war-neuroses – their nature and significance. *Psycho-Analytic Studies of the Personality*. (London: Tavistock, 1952).

Fountain, G. (2000). The potential space in the psychoanalytic situations: Considerations regarding the structure and dynamic of the analytic process on the basis of two-person psychology. *Psychoanalytic Quarterly*, 69:440.

Freud, S. (1924). The Dissolution of the Oedipus Complex, SE Vol. 19, pp 173–179. 1931 [1974] Female Sexuality. *In Standard Edition of the Complete Psychological Works of Sigmund Freud*, Vol. 21, J. Strachey, ed. pp. 221–243. London: Hogarth Press.

Gray, E.D. (1982). *Patriarchy as a conceptual trap*. Wellesley, MA: Roundtable Press.

Hays, S. (1996). *The cultural contradictions of motherhood*. New Haven, CT: Yale University Press.

Hoffnung, M. (1989). Motherhood: Contemporary conflict for women. In J. Freeman (Ed.), *Women: A feminist perspective* (4th ed. pp. 157–175). Mountain View: CA: Mayfield.

Johnston-Robledo, I. (2000). From post-partum depression to the empty nest syndrome. The motherhood mystique revisited. In J.C. Chrisler, G. Golden, & P.D. Rozee (Eds.), *Lectures on the psychology of women* (pp. 129–148). Boston: McGraw-Hill.

June, M. (2004). *Offering Flowers, Feeding Skulls: Popular Goddess Worship in West Bengal*, Oxford University Press.

Klein, M. (1937). Love, guilt and reparation. In *Love, Guilt and Reparation and Other Works 1921–1945* (1988). Virago Press Ltd.

Klein, M. (1975a) [1935]. A Contribution to the Psychogenesis of Manic-Depressive States. In: *The Writings of Melanie Klein*, Vol. 1, R.E. Money Kyrle, B. Joseph, E.O. Shaughnessy, and H. Segal, eds., London: Hogarth Press and the Institute of Psychoanalysis.

Klein, M. (1975b) [1930]. The Importance of Symbol Formation in the Development of the Ego. In *The Writings of Melanie Klein*, Vol. 1 R.E. Money Kyrle, B. Joseph, E.O. Shaughnessy, and H. Segal, eds., London: Hogarth Press and the Institute of Psychoanalysis.

Lacan, J. (1964). *Le seminaire 11: les quarter concepts fondamentaux de la psychanalyse* [Seminar 11: The four fundamental concepts of psychoanalysis]. Paris: Editions du Seuil.

Levi-Strauss, C. (1956). *The Family, in Man, Culture and Society*. Shapiro, H.L. (Ed.), Paris: Oxford University Press, p. 274.

Lorber, J. (1993b). *Paradoxes of gender*. New Haven, CT: Yale University Press.

Makowski, J.F. (1985). Persephone. Psyche, and the mother-maiden archetype. *The Classical Outlook*, 62, 3 (March–April):73–78.

McMahon, M. (1995). *Engendering motherhood*. New York: Guildford.

Neumann, E. (1955). *The Great Mother*. Trans. Ralph Manheim. Princeton: Princeton University Press.

Oakley, A. (1974). *The sociology of housework*. New York: Pantheon.

Raphael-Leff, J. (1989). Where the wild things are. *International Journal of Prenatal and Perinatal Studies*, 1:79–89.

Rossi, A. (1977). A Biosocial Perspective on Parenting. *Daedalus*, 106(2):1–32.

Rothbaum, F., Rosen, K., Ujiie, T., & Uchida, N. (2002). *Family Process*, 41, 3:328–350.

Seymour, S. (1999). *Women, family and childcare in India: A world in transition*. Cambridge: Cambridge University Press.

Spitz, R.A. (1957). *No and Yes.* (New York: Int. Univ. Press.)

Stern, D.N. (1995). Maternal representations: A clinical and subjective phenomenological view. *Infant Mental Health Journal*, 12(3):175–186.

Thompson, W.I. (1981). *The time falling bodies take to light*. New York: St. Martin's.

Winnicott, D.W. (1956). Primary maternal preoccupation. In *Through Paediatrics to Psychoanalysis* (1982). London: Hogarth Press.

Winnicott, D.W. (1958). The capacity to be alone. *The International Journal of Psychonalysis*, 39:416–420.

Winnicott, D.W. (1960). The relationship of a mother to her baby at the beginning. In *The Family and Individual Development* (1965). London: Tavistock.

Winnicott, D.W. (1965). *The Maturational Processes and the Facilitating Environment*. London: Hogarth Press.

Winnicott, D.W. (1967). The Location of Cultural Experience. In *Playing and Reality*. London: Penguin Books.

Winnicott, D.W. (1971). *Playing and Reality*. Middlesex: Penguin.

Part III

Introduction to the Seduction of Religion

Jhuma Basak

Religion and mythology have always played a very pivotal role in Indian society, its people, and their psychic structure. At times, as a decisive and cementing agent, or at times a divisive force provoking a voice of resistance. And often it may even continue to hold an archaic validation in the collective unconscious. In this sense religion may also operate as a 'container' for human agony. While mythology contributes to the creation of the community's cultural fantasies and imagination.

The first paper in this section, *The Role of Religious Icons and Mythological Figures in Traumatized Individuals: A Psychoanalytic Perspective,* by Monisha Nayar-Akhtar, expands the connection between myths, psychoanalysis and its socio-cultural contexts. In respect to that Nayar-Akhtar inspects the perpetual negligence of mythologies from the Far East, Middle East, and South Asian regions. Subsequently she upholds her argument of such regions continuing to "living myth" rather than myths merely "portraying fiction" (Doniger).

Expanding on Jacob Arlow's exposition that "myth is a particular kind of communal experience," Nayar-Akhtar gradually weaves in the ego's journey with myths from a community cooperative point to a 'personal myth' (Kris). Further, how myths may act as a "culturally adaptive solution to developmental conflicts through identification with the mythical characters" (Balter). To finally establish her theoretical speculation, Nayar-Akhtar narrates from a clinical vignette, Kamala.

The second paper in this section, *Mourning over Karbala: Rethinking Ritual Actions of Shia Women in Kolkata,* by Epsita Halder, unfolds the narrative of ritualistic mourning embedded in Muharram, that carries the painful legend of the sacrifice of Imam Husayn, the grandson of the Prophet, in the battle of Karbala.

In continuation of the story of Husayn's martyrdom, Zaynab, the sister of Husayn, led the women to Medina to grieve the loss of male kinsfolk in the battle of Karbala. Zaynab and Sakina, the daughter of Husayn, became the leading grieving voices of the loss from Karbala. In Muharram, the public act of lamenting by self-flagellation with chains is only for the men to perform while the women's site of mourning resides in the overlapping space of their daily living and a larger site of contestation. The Shia women are like a minority-within-minority community in Kolkata. It is said that the conflict between the Sunnis and the Shias within the Muslim community in Bengal goes back to the colonial times. In respect to that Halder cites the exile of Wajid Ali Shah from his kingdom Lucknow by the British in 1856, and his eventual settlement in the fringes of Calcutta (Metiabruz area) giving rise to the subsequent flow of urban flow of Shias gathering around close proximity of the Sunnis. And in this way Halder elaborates the creation of a 'ghetto within the Muslim ghetto.'

The journey through Halder's paper ponders over women's capacity of 'acting' within given religious norms – it reflects over 'gendered acting' within the religious practice of a common community loss that affects both men and women equally. The paper examines the growing changes in time and how religious traditional norms are giving way to 'innovative agency' of Shia women's practice within the religious domain.

4 The role of religious icons and mythological figures in traumatised individuals: A psychoanalytic perspective

Monisha C. Nayar-Ahktar

Man, mythology, and religion

People's relationship with myths is ubiquitous and ancient. Created by humans and reflecting the richness of human cultural fantasies and imagination, myths with their accompanying historical icons and legends are seen as answers to existential anxieties that have plagued man throughout history. Numerous definitions of myths all seem to have some things in common. They are all concerned with people's captivation with the meaning of their origin and their lives as well as their relationship with the supernatural, past, and future (Anastasopoulos, Soumaki, & Anagnostopoulos, 2010; Mohacsy, 2001). Reflecting worries over time, they evolve and are universal, though culturally contextualised and function to contain anxieties, worries, and fears at particular times (Bruner, 1959).

While myths were seen as having metaphysical, cosmological, sociological, and psychological functions, it was the last function that was seen as being the most fundamental one (Gullestad, 1995; Pietikainen, 1999). The psychological function provides an "explanation of the world that conveys meaning and that contributes to sustaining human institutions" (Gullestad, 1995, 1156). Not surprisingly, it has engrossed the minds of psychoanalysts as well beginning with Freud, whose discovery of the Oedipus complex paid homage to ancient Greek mythologies while defining the central tenet of psychoanalytic theory itself. However, the plethora of mythologies of the Far East, Middle East, and South Asian regions was largely ignored. In these regions, myths continue to shape cultures and speak to realities instead of 'portraying fiction' (Perennis, (1993), p. 3) to which the Greek and other Western mythologies, 'de-mythologized' (Perennis, (1993), p. 3) as they were, had been for the most part relegated. According to Perennis, (1993) there is "no better way to understand the structure of mythical thought than to study cultures in which myth is a 'living thing' constituting the very support of religious life" (p. 3). This paper expands on the idea of a 'living myth' (Perennis, (1993), p. 3) and explores the intricate connection between these myths, psychoanalysis, and the socio-cultural context in which they live and breathe.

Let me expand on this further within the context of psychoanalysis.

Psychoanalysis and mythology

The study of myths in psychoanalysis begins with Freud's early and lifelong fascination with myths. Freud (1900) gives a central place to the myth of Oedipus in this theory and placed it in a position of prominence in his meta-psychology. Freud defined it as the universal characteristic of early childhood of all males (though Freud attempted to formulate this for females as well, it has been challenged and alternative perspectives on female development proposed (Gilligan, 1982; Bernstein, 2001; Chasseguet-Smirgel, 1988; Kulish & Holtzman, 1998; Chasseguet-Smirgel, 1999). Freud stated that the successful resolution of this conflict was quintessential to ameliorating neurotic suffering (Boehm, 1931; Goldberg, 1989). This discovery was pivotal and central to the development of Freud's psychoanalytic theory. The play only served to provide a skeletal frame within which Freud masterfully crafted the quintessential features of the Oedipal conflict (guilt, envy, desire, and fear).

Psychoanalysis and religion

Despite Freud's apparent use of Greek myths in his theorizing, his relationship with religion was rather complex. Traditionally pathologizing and marginalizing religion, Freud was critical of the childish illusions (later termed *delusions*) underlying religious belief. According to Freud, two childhood wishes or psychological needs lead to the construction of religious beliefs.

1)   Having to come to terms with their complicated emotions towards their father and,
2)   A child's sense of helplessness in the face of the danger of the outer and inner worlds.

Nevertheless, in subsequent years several theorists emphasized how rituals in religious experiences serve as a means for a healthy accommodation of the repression of desire demanded by all cultures and civilizations. Within this contextual framework, ritual behavior is a product of the nonpathological and often beneficial mechanism of suppression not repression.

While the legend of Oedipus Rex gave impetus to Freud's seminal contributions regarding the nature of childhood sexuality, psychoanalytic exploration of myths remained for the most part sparse and sketchy. It was only in the mid-1960s that a seminal paper by Jacob Arlow on ego-psychology and myths increased interest in this topic and expanded further upon the educational and clinical functions of myths in general. Arlow's paper formed the basis for a conference on this topic, the first of its kind in the psychoanalytic arena. Arlow (1961) wrote:

> Psychoanalysis has a greater contribution to make to the study of mythology than demonstrating, in myths, wishes often encountered in

the unconscious thinking of patients. The myth is a particular kind of communal experience. It is a special form of shared fantasy and its serves to bring the individual into relationship with members of his cultural group on the basis of certain common needs. Accordingly, the myth can be studied from the point of view of its function in psychic integration – how it plays a role in warding off feelings of guilt and anxiety how it constituted a form of adaptation to reality and to the group in which the individual lives and how it influences the crystallization of the individual identity and the formation of the superego. (p. 375)

Arlow's (1961) objective was simple. By applying ego psychology to the study of myths, he hoped to establish a frame of reference whereby the study of mythology could be further validated. By equating myths with dreams and the symbolism inherent in this analogy leading to an examination of both manifest and latent content (Balter, 1969; Freud, 1900; Grolnick, 1984). Arlow (1961) stated how symbolism could be used to find new and latent meanings in the manifest content of the myth itself. Having described myths as a universally shared fantasy, Arlow (1961) elaborates on what constitutes unconscious fantasy thinking. He refers to it as a "form of mental function ... [that] is dynamically related to the persistent cathectic potential emanating from the pressure of the instinctual wishes of the id" (Arlow, 1961, p. 375). He goes on to illuminate the role of the ego to contain and facilitate discharge and/or expression in an adaptive, integrated manner consistent with external reality and avoiding anxiety emanating from intrapsychic conflict.

The unconscious life

Unconscious fantasy thinking, of which internalisation of cultural myths can be a part, is therefore one attempt by the ego to provide integration for the institutional demands of the id. The demands on the ego to incorporate, integrate, correlate, and adapt to internal pressures and external realities leads to the creation of myths, dreams, symptoms, and fantasies (Arlow, 1961). Fantasy life is considered to be often hierarchical in psychic organisation reflecting "the vicissitudes of individual experiences as well as the influence of psychic differentiation and ego development" (Arlow, 1961, p. 377). The ego functions to integrate infantile wishes, exhibit both adaptive and defensive responsibilities (Arlow, 1961). Unconscious fantasies, can often be hierarchically grouped, serving as a "psychic moment" (Arlow, 1961, p. 377) in the history of the individual's development. The ego's defensive functions may also serve to group certain fantasies which act to repudiate other fantasies (often disturbing) from the individual's past. These more acceptable fantasies now serve as powerful narratives which are accepted and experienced as realities from the past. Kris (1956) describes this as the "personal myth" (p. 654). Referring to a "biographical self-image," the personal myth is "not only ... an essential part of [some individuals'] self-representation, but it has become a treasured possession to which the patient is attached with a peculiar devotion" (Kris, 1956, p. 654). Over time, this term denoted central themes or fantasies emerging in psychoanalysis allowing for the construction of a narrative that allows them to subvert a perceived destiny (Gullestad, 1995).

The organization of an individual's unconscious fantasy life continues to occur over the course of his/her development. Clinically, as Arlow (1961) noted, one can see the defensive and hierarchical use of myths and fantasies to screen out an earlier integrated unconscious fantasy. According to Arlow (1961), the shift from individual fantasy and personal myths to shared fantasies and cultural communal myth relies on the idea that "shared daydreams and myths are instruments of socialization" (p. 379). Myths as instruments of socialization is echoed by Bruner's (1960) notion of the metaphoric identity. Serving as role models, these myths allow for both defensive and adaptive uses. Occurring in the context of personal daydreams, they are meant to be forgotten. But in the context of a cultural myth they can be repeated and collectively remembered and analyzed. They can serve to contain daily anxiety and impulses through societally sanctioned meaning, art, and symbolism (as present in mythologies) and through the use of externalization and/ or projection, allowing the individual to connect to and evolve with idealized cultural constructions of their social world.

In bringing ego psychology to bear on the understanding of myths Arlow (1961) and others (Kakar, 1989; Kris, 1956), demonstrated the unique psychological qualities and social functioning potential of personal and cultural myths. Using ego psychology as a conceptual base, he elaborated and elucidated the adaptive nature of myths especially during "particular 'psychic moment[s]' in ontogenetic development" (Balter, 1969, p. 218). Arlow along with others, considered myths as "culturally adaptive solutions to developmental conflicts through identifications with the mythical characters" (Balter, 1969, p. 218). These ego psychologists expanded on how an individual's intrapsychic struggle can be externalized in the myth (taking the form of shared fantasies) then reintegrated and used adaptively in the resolution of developmental conflicts.

The contributions of the ego psychologists along with advances in psychoanalytic theory (including affect, the relational realm in analytic work, and the inclusion of culture and society and advances in female psychology) further opened the door to a reexamination of myths. As the psychoanalytic discourse surrounding myths continued to expand to include myths from the Far East and South Asian region, contemporary perspectives on myths and their functions became far more complex and nuanced. Adding to this literary conundrum Doniger's (1992) notion of myths as "fiction" (p. 3) (e.g., Greek myths which have become demythologized) and myths that can be considered as "living" (p. 3) (those that continue to operate in daily living and societal structures) suggest that contemporary understanding of how myths operate in everyday day and clinical populations may need reexamination. In fact one might say a wider net may need to be cast to understand their significance.

One such perspective gaining momentum in the psychoanalytic arena addresses the role of myths in the development of personal and adolescent identity. In a 2010 paper by Anastasopoulos, Soumaki, and Anagnostopoulos, the relationship between adolescence and mythology is explored in depth. These authors expand on earlier notions of myths as being integral to the developmental process and especially during the phase of identity development. They elaborate on the need for heroes and personal and spiritual models for identification as a quintessential feature of adolescence, along with the need to idealize and explain the profound physiological changes occurring in the body. The second individuation process, described by Blos, (1967) as capturing the turbulent intrapsychic conflicts during adolescence, can draw upon cultural and societal structures (as in myths and heroes) to contain and metabolize normal adult responsibilities and also overwhelming feelings of despair, loneliness, and pain. How they shape the development of the self, are integrated into their lives, and become part of their identity is a matter of ongoing speculation and further inquiry. One line of inquiry lies in further exploration of the constructive function that Arlow (1961), Gullestad (1995), and others envisioned for the role of religious experience and mythology in identity formation, one that solidified the role of myths as "instruments of socialization" (Arlow, 1961:379). Mythical images and models (heroes, prophets, and legends) serve as ego ideals that the individual strives towards. This 'range of metaphoric identity' as subsumed in myths (Bruner, 1959) is critical to individual identity development and its presence during adolescence perhaps ubiquitous.

The development and resolution of identity is often described as occurring during normal ontological transitions from infant to childhood, adolescence, and young adulthood. However, as an ongoing construction process, identity can and should continue to change, re-crystallize, and in other words, develop throughout the life-span especially during periods of socio-cultural, geo-political transitions or crises.

Myths in a cultural context

Like all groups, immigrant communities, especially those coming from old-world and traditional societies, bring with them a rich milieu of religious, historical, mythological heritage that make up their sense of self and are used to frame, build, and repair ongoing identity construction. South Asian immigrant communities provide clear examples of people actively referencing, reflecting, and applying historical or mythological stories to life events, using them to interpret opportunities and difficulties, to guide personal action, and to assimilate experiences into self-development. Modern mythical beliefs can include references to figures with some general corroborative historical support (The Buddha, Jesus Christ, the Prophet Mohammad) that are endowed with supernatural qualities or can include literary figures existing on a pure supernatural plane (e.g., Angel Gabriel, Indian Pantheon of deities). Kakar

(1982) vividly describes the role of religious and mythological icons in the life of a South Asian in his psychoanalytically informed explication of the Indian psyche. He writes:

> The roles of myths, especially those of religious derivation, in defining and integrating the traditional elements and the common features of identity and society in Hindu India cannot be over-estimated. Myths, on one sense are individual psychology projected onto the outside world; they let what is actually going on 'inside' happen 'outside'. Myths not only convey communal versions of the repressed wishes and fantasies of early childhood, functioning as a kind of deep freeze for socially unacceptable impulses; they also reflect the nature of individual's interpersonal bonds within his culture. They are a kind of collective historical conscience. (p. 4)

While recognizing the various ways that myths can be analyzed and utilized, Kakar's (1982) focus is on the psychosocial framework. For a South Asian, or any actively practicing religious person for that matter, whose external life is often imbued with mythology and religion (as in daily practice, rituals, religious text reading and recitation, folklore storytelling, devotional songs, etc.), the constructed meanings may be internalized as part of their identity. For such a person, mythological and religious icons are often synonymous, exerting a multilayered influence on the individual, throughout their development and life-span. Through a process of emulation, incorporation, introjection, and identification, aspects of these myths and the religious icons along with their various interpretations may become part of person's inner realities. The juxtaposition of religion and mythology was also expanded upon by Arlow (1961) who disagreed with earlier studies of religion and rituals. Earlier explorations of religion and rituals in communities (Freud, 1913), which reduced them to the functional status of obsessional neurosis, were according to Arlow (1961), "too narrow a framework to view of richness of religious experience" (p. 387). Unfortunately, this perspective was not widely accepted in the psychoanalytic community and the ego-syntonic nature of these mythological and religious icons and their internal representations may therefore have been lost on the Western-trained analyst unfamiliar with the religious cultures of their clients and its role in collective historical conscience. If such associations do appear in treatment, they may not be understood, attempts may be made to analyse them away, and their adaptive functions in an individual's life may be confused with defensive underpinnings. Increased migration and globalization of health has accelerated both the awareness of the epic nature of mental illness and health as well as the need to explore functional ways to address them in clinical practice. Examining the scope of religious beliefs and icons in personal development is beyond the scope of the paper though its significance in the integration of a South Asian identity cannot be denied and will need further exploration.

Briefly on trauma

This brief overview on myths, religious practices, and its integration in intrapsychic functions suggests an overall evolving trend of integration and adaptation. The analysis of personal myths and shared fantasies of any individual would then provide the analyst with a rich array of analytic material to understand the intrapsychic world of the analysand and her/his particular manner of conflict resolution and adaptation.

The role of myths and religious beliefs in the containment of personal anxieties and in the resolution of one's conflicts and its contribution to personal identity formation and intrapsychic integration can now lead one to question its potential role in the resolution and integration of significant trauma.

The following vignette examines how certain myths and their icons become integrated into the fabric of one's personal identity and form the scaffolding to cope with individual traumas. The analytic process allows two people to engage in an understanding of a complex process that can be facilitated by understanding the cultural myths of the patient's society. The process can yield both the adaptive and defensive aspects of these representations, which can then be understood by the analytic dyad and within the analytic space with all its transferential and defensive underpinnings.

Case of Kamala

The myth of Durga, as the Goddess of Strength (Shakti), is ancient in large parts of Indian folklore. There are several myths regarding the Goddess and her various attributes from her ascending to a celestial abode to those that describe her transformation from the Goddess Durga to the Goddess Kali. What follows is a particular Bengali folklore that is widely celebrated in Bengal during the fall months and referred to as 'Durga Puja.'

According to this Bengali folklore, Durga, then known as Uma was born the daughter of a local King. Uma spent her early childhood and young adolescent life, praying fervently to obtain the hand of the Lord Shiva whose powers as the Divine Presence were legendary. Practicing self-discipline, denial, and asceticism for many years, Uma eventually won the hand of Shiva, the God of Destruction/Transformation in the Hindu Trinity. After ascending to her heavenly abode, Uma now known as Durga, whose name is synonymous with Shaki (strength), Janaki, and Parvati, lived an idyllic life bearing four children with her husband. However, as mortals are often known to do, longings to see her mother and visit her maternal home ultimately arose. The Goddess' descent to her earthly home became a yearly tradition celebrated throughout India in a variety of ways. The festival is celebrated with great pomp. They typically show Durga in a fierce and combative posture, depicting the beheading of the demon, Mahisha. She is accompanied by her four children, Kartik and Ganesh (her sons) and Saraswati and Laxmi (her two daughters). The visual image of Durga inspires reverence, awe, piety, and love in all who attend the ceremonies.

Kamala, a professional South Asian woman in her 30s, sought treatment when she became depressed and anxious following the sudden demise of her ailing mother. Kamala had migrated to the United States about 20 years ago from her native country, India, when she got married. Moving from her homeland to another country had stirred up many feelings of alienation and loneliness though she appeared to have adapted and was now the mother of three children. According to Kamala, her symptoms were not recent as she was experiencing marital difficulties as well. Though she had attempted to obtain help for these difficulties, they remained unaddressed for several reasons. Kamala hobbled along in her life, pursuing her career objectives, which while satisfying, did nothing to ameliorate the loneliness and despair that she felt from time to time. The sudden death of her mother added to an already painful situation and Kamala found herself unable to cope and manage her day-to-day life.

According to Kamala, she had always enjoyed a very special relationship with her mother. She was the youngest of four children and dearly loved by her mother. As the only girl, her position was also unique and her attachment to her mother grew unchecked and unabated till she was 2 years old. At that time, her mother became depressed, and was unable to take care of young Kamala. As the youngest of four children, with several years between herself and her next oldest sibling, Kamala found herself quite alone, abandoned, and confused about the sudden absence of her loving mother. Her father, a busy professional man, had little time for his daughter as did her siblings who gradually drifted away from the family. Envied by her brothers for her closeness to her mother, Kamala was now a victim of their verbal and physical abuse and neglect. Kamala was 5 years old when her mother recovered (after a long period of psychiatric treatment). She could now begin to reengage with Kamala, offering her the love that she had desperately longed for. Kamala began to blossom once again with this care though certain adaptive defenses gradually began to be more noticeable and rigid. However, despite the mother's return to relative normalcy, she remained emotionally vulnerable and weak, susceptible to the taunts of her domineering husband and now Kamala's older siblings as well. This fact was not lost on young Kamala who remained ever vigilant of her mother's changing moods and fragile emotional state. Her defenses over time served her well though at a cost that we could only begin to understand gradually during the course of our work.

In her treatment, Kamala identified these as her 'stoic look' and denial of any suffering. While there were many significant aspects of her treatment, it was Kamala's focus on the worship of two deities that became central to the work of her analysis. These were the Mother Goddesses, Durga and Kali. Kamala's mother, a devout Hindu, was an avid worshipper of these two Goddesses and Kamala grew up hearing the mythological lore surrounding these religious figures. The ones that appealed to young Kamala were the ones where the Goddess Durga, also known as the Goddess of Strength, vanquishes the demon God Mahisha. The Goddess Kali, who is also seen as another representation of Durga, is also endowed with significant powers. The myths and tales of their endowed powers were intricately woven into the fabric of her upbringing. Her mother's worship of Kali, at home, added to a young girl's growing feeling that the Goddess was a powerful and empowering woman who unlike her mother had the power to vanquish and destroy all enemies.

Kamala's later worship of these deities and her exploration of these myths revealed her attempts to integrate, adapt, and defend against the painful external realities of her life. Her experience of herself as a strong and contained woman, yet one who could explode and wreak havoc, had sustained her during her adolescent years and early adulthood when her mother's mental health deteriorated and she was once again hospitalized. Kamala did not turn to her friends (who never knew of her mother's illness) nor did she talk to her family. Her mother's history of illness and recovery continued for several years. Kamala attended to her mother, remaining psychologically and physically close to her. With her marriage, a physical separation ensued, but though her contact with her mother diminished, her emotional wounds continued to fester inside eventually leading her to seek treatment. In her private and professional life, Kamala had built walls that were impenetrable leading to a false illusion of safety and containment for herself and alienation from others as a result. Her marital difficulties could now be at least partly viewed within this context.

During the course of her analysis, Kamala began to understand her internal representations of the Mother Goddess Durga and Kali. By holding onto her belief (albeit defensively) that she had incredible strength, she had been able to adapt and cope to a life of neglect and abuse. Lulled by an adaptive identification with the Goddesses, Kamala believed that she could vanquish anything, even her own needs and internal demons as she put it. Her strong identification with the Goddess of Strength had led to a denial of her personal needs and feelings. Gradually, she could begin to reclaim hitherto repudiated parts of herself, and as she did, her ability to tolerate the pain of the realization of her losses increased. Kamala could then begin to mourn the parts of her mother she never had. With this process, Kamala could begin to recognise her own aggression and strength and the defensive yet adaptive identifications she had maintained with both Goddesses. Their legendary presence in her community had found its way into her early ego functioning and became an impenetrable shield of armor as she grew into a young woman.

Discussion

In this paper, I examine how myths and religious beliefs are integrated as part of personal development and identity formation in the case of some patients. The vignette describes how a particular myth can become part of inner reality and help organize in constructive or obstructive ways, a person's approach to navigating tasks and experiences. During treatment, this patient could consciously recall and talk about her external reality and connect it to the past personal history of family trauma and to religious doctrines and beliefs. Despite the external reality, she was aware of how religious beliefs and associated myths had shaped her life and identity. It was during the course of the analytic process, with further exploration, that we could begin to understand to some extent how her lived life was a reflection of her allegiance to a particular Hindu tradition and the religious ideals and myths associated with them. Her inner reality, both conscious and unconscious, within a socio-cultural context, could be understood as attempts to defend against and adapt to painful affects in her traumatic pasts.

The implications of this for understanding personal development are several. It continues to provide support for the idea that the rich, long history of religious figures and mythological icons found in South Asian and other so-cieties can serve as large yet malleable containers of complex, adaptively constructive affect. Their holding and containing functions, recognized (in the literature) by others as well (Arlow, 1961; Perennis, (1993); Kakar, 1982), are often experienced as critical parts of one's identity and are actively used as guides in navigating not just crises, but everyday life questions and issues.

The uninformed analyst/therapist might overlook the significance of their use to the patient and by attempting to analyse away or 'demythologize' the organizing associations to religious deities and rituals, runs the risk of a potential impasse in treatment. This can lead to alienating these groups from seeking professional mental health services here or in their home countries. While it is true that there could be defensive aspects of such integrations as we saw in the case of Kamala, it is also true that there were adaptive aspects to these identifications that were part of their cultural upbringing, and that had served them in positive ways. It is only during the course of an empathic and informed treatment that one can learn to play with those sublimated parts to develop them into better adaptive tools for the patient's continued progress. It is evident that Kamala benefited from treatment that did not dismantle her inner realities through application of a traditional and precise analytic lens. Instead, a more contemporary approach, informed by notions of Indian self and the role of myths, served to anchor such individuals in their treatment. The development of identity, and one informed by religious belief and mythology served as powerful conceptual containers for the therapist as well as provided an emotional scaffolding for the patient in her development.

References

Anastasopoulos, D., Soumaki, E., & Anagnostopoulos, D. (2010). Adolescence and mythology. *Journal of Child Psychotherapy*, 36:119:132.

Arlow, J.A. (1961). Ego psychology and the study of mythology. *Journal of the American Psychoanalytic Association*, 9:371–393.

Armstrong, K. (2004). *Buddha*. New York, NY: Viking Press.

Atkins, N.B. (1970). The Oedipus myth, adolescence, and the succession of generations. *Journal of American Psychoanalytic Association*, 18:860–875.

Balter, L. (1969). The mother as source of power a psychoanalytic study of three Greek myths. *Psychoanalytic Quarterly*, 38:217–274.

Bernstein, A. (2001). Freud and Oedipus: a new look at the Oedipus complex in the light of Freud's life. *Modern Psychoanalysis*, 26:269–282.

Blos, P. (1967). The second individuation process of adolescence. *Psychoanalytic Study of the Child*, 22:162–186.

Bruner, J.S. (1959). Myth and identity. *Daedalus: Myth and Mythmaking*, 88(2):349–358.

Boehm, F. (1931). The history of the Oedipus complex. *International Journal of Psycho-analysis*, 12:431–451.

Chasseguet-Smirgel, J. (1988). From the archaic matrix of the Oedipus complex to the fully developed Oedipus complex – theoretical perspective in relation to clinical experience and technique. *Psychoanalytic Quarterly*, 57:505–527.

Chasseguet-Smirgel, J. (1999). Oedipus and Psyche. *British Journal of Psychoanalysis*, 15:465–475.

Freud, S. (1913). *Totem and taboo: Some points of agreement between the mental lives of savages and neurotics.* London: Hogarth Press.

Freud, S. (1900). *The interpretation of dreams. Standard Edition.* London: Hogarth Press.

Freud, S. (1928). *The future of an illusion. Standard Edition.* London: Hogarth Press.

Freud, S. (1930). *Civilization and its discontents. Standard Edition.* London: Hogarth Press.

Gilligan, D. (1982). *In a different voice.* Cambridge, MA: Harvard University Press.

Goldberg, C. (1989). The shame of Hamlet and Oedipus. *Psychoanalytic Review*, 76:581–603.

Grolnick, S.A. (1984). Play, myth, theater, and psychoanalysis. *Psychoanalytic Review*, 71:247–262.

Gullestad, S.E. (1995). The personal myth as a clinical concept. *International Journal of Psycho-analysis*, 76:1155–1166.

Kakar, S. (1979). *Indian childhood: Cultural ideals and social reality.* New Delhi, India: Oxford University Press (Oxford India Paperbacks).

Kakar, S. (1982). *A psycho-analytic study of childhood society in India.* New Delhi, India: Oxford University Press (Oxford India Paperbacks).

Kakar, S. (1989). The maternal-feminine in Indian psychoanalysis. *International Review of Psycho-analysis*, 16:355–362.

Kris, E. (1956). The personal myth – a problem in psychoanalytic technique. *Journal of the American Psychoanalytic Association*, 4:653–681.

Kulish, N. & Holtzman, D. (1998). Persephone, the Loss of Virginity and the Female Oedipal Complex. *Int. J. Psycho-Anal.* 79:57–71.

Maguire, J. (2001). *Essential Buddhism: A complete guide to beliefs and practices.* New York, NY: Simon & Schuster - Atria Books.

Mohacsy, I. (2001). The currency of mythology. *Journal of the American Academy of Psychoanalysis*, 29:649–658.

Pietikainen, P. (1999). Jung's psychology in the light of his 'personal myth'. *Psychoanalytic History*, 1:237–251.

Perennis, P. (1993). *Reciprocity and Transformation in Hindu and Jaina Texts Paperback* Ed. Wendy Doninger, Albany, NY: State University of New York Press.

5 Mourning over Karbala: Rethinking ritual actions of Shia women in Kolkata

Epsita Halder

On the day of *Ashura*, the tenth of the month of Muharram, Shia men emerge from their imambaras (ritual site for congregation and mourning) in grand processions, lamenting over the martyrdom of Imam Husayn, the grandson of the Prophet, in the battle of Karbala in 680 CE. They carry the decorated *taziyeh* (the replica of Imam Husayn's grave), chant *marsiya/nawha* (elegy) with vigorous *sineh-jani* (chest beating), and at the moment of utter ecstasy that only pain brings, they engage in *janjeer-jani* –the spectacular self-flagellation with chains that end in razors cutting deep into the flesh of their chests and backs. Though women are never part of such public displays of pain, they follow the procession which goes from the local imambara to the ultimate destination – Karbala – a nearby place revered as the symbolic battleground of martyrdom. Women are an active and integral part of the commemoration of Muharram that starts before the procession with fasts and lament rituals inside the *imambara*s. In the private lament rituals, the grieving voices of the women of the *ahlul bayt* (the family of the Prophet) who lost their men in Karbala are invoked in the elegies which men and women chant, beating their chests all the while.

In the beginning of the month of Muharram, the cityscape suddenly changes with the collective public appearance of Shia women in their black mourning attire, going to and fro their homes and imambaras. Such ritual journeys through the everyday regular urban spaces make them visible as Shia women whose identities otherwise remain indistinguishable from the overall gendered Muslim public. At the same time, such movements in the name of Imam Husayn enable them to get access over and manoeuvre public space and in the process transform them as actors of the space. This essay will discuss how the Shia women, through their ritual actions, transform the sacred space that they inhabit and how they work on that allotted space to perform modes of 'place-making' (Desplat, 2012). This essay tries to understand the semantic specificities of the site of women's mourning ritual and its contextual configurations to understand the sacred site both as a space of living and a larger site of contestation.[1]

Shias are a minority-within-minority community (Sachedina, 1994:3–14). In the Indian context and their private enactment of lament and public performance of pain offer a critical point to understand the emotional, material, and political context of the community's double minority status with its rival claims over the Prophetic inheritance in a Hindu-majoritarian state. Women's ritual actions are not only embedded in the community's constant conflict-within with the Sunni hegemonic religiosity,[2] their functions are actually meaningful in the context of the community's constant negotiations with the state for acceptance and recognition. Hence a re-affirmation, both as Muslims and as Shia-minority becomes inevitable to gain legitimacy for their sectarian identity within, and for reformulating public perception of their form of devotion mainly visible during Muharram.

Here, I will concentrate on the ritual activities of the Twelver Shias[3] in Kolkata based on my ethnographic research between 2011 and 2013. What I propose here is women's ritual actions cannot be separated from the actions of the community as a collective that are at once trans-territorial in essence and nationally demarcated. At the same time it is regionally located and linguistically identified. Such an argument will place Shia women's ritual action as integral to the broader question of the Shia community in Kolkata which has so far remained unexplored as a religious-cultural phenomenon. It will also complicate their double-marginalisation by amining other micro-contexts along which the community functions.

The public procession of Muharram on the day of Ashura alarmingly instigates sectarian tensions at times. Clashes have broken out between the Sunnis and the Shias necessitating state intervention and surveillance since the colonial times (Cole, 1988:115). For being a double minority in a non-Islamic Indian sub-continent, to the Shias such administrative surveillance comes as a form of administrative security. Such control only makes Muharram commemoration viable as a public ritual and ensures access over the public space as an inherent part of community rights.

Migrant Shia communities in a Bengali Hindu Kolkata:

The Shias have settled in Kolkata as a result of long, intermittent, and multiple strands of internal regional migration of Shia families from north India, and slow and subsequent conversion and intermixing in Bengal. The ruler Wajid Ali Shah's exile from his kingdom in Lucknow to the southern fringes of colonial Calcutta (in 1856) after the Shia state of Awadh was captured by the British resulted in his creating a mini Lucknow in Metiabruz with more migration of elites and artisans. The subsequent flow of the Shias from north Indian states such as Uttar Pradesh and Bihar and their settlements in various quarters of Kolkata show a pattern of urban settlement in ghetto-like economic fringes where they live in close proximity to the Sunnis or other ethnic and regional groups. These groups are mostly poor or lower middle class, and mostly migrants. Being Shias, the community feels constant threats of invalidation in a Sunni locality, creating a ghetto within the Muslim ghetto. The Shia sacred imambara and forms of devotional performance are pushed to the margins of Muslim devotionalism in a mosque-centric religious culture. As a result, the Shia ethics of grieving and forms of performing pain in inconspicuous imambaras in the bylanes remain obscure and unintelligible to the non-Muslim population.

The question of civic safety is embedded in the pain of Muharram and cannot be dissociated from its performance. It is always fraught, for its capacity to attract Sunni apathy confines the regular performances inside the security of the imambaras. Though the Ripon Street areas (between Park Circus and Maulali) have not demonstrated any direct sectarian confrontation recently or recorded any negative campaign against the Shias, the overarching presence of such insecurity as the core of their sacred activity and everyday mobility is perhaps based on a trans-historical experience of persecution, and multi-local instances of Sunni-Shia clashes during Muharram. To be able to gather at an imambara, then, becomes emotionally and socially enabling, and surrendering to Imam Husayn as Muslims and as Shias. This creates a sense of security in a Sunni-dominated ghetto and a Bengali Hindu public sphere.

Imam Husayn's sacrifice and his sister Zaynab: Martyrdom and gender

After the martyrdom of Husayn in Karbala with his small band of army the women and children of Prophet's family were taken to Damesque as war prisoners. Once the women and children of *ahlul bayt* were released from captivity, Zaynab, the sister of Imam Husayn, sent a message to the community at the public square of Damascus to not to forget the dishonour and persecution that the family of the Prophet faced. She consolidated a community – of the Shias – as the follower of Imam Husayn. She also led the women enroute to Medina to lament over the martyred male kinsfolk in the battlefield of Karbala. Zaynab's voice and form of grieving have remained the base for the ethics of loyalty and textualization of elegies and lament (Hyder, 2006:161–183). The grieving voices of women – mostly of Husayn's sister Zaynab and daughter Sakina – are emulated and their distress narrated to invoke a tremendous sense of loss which both men and women perform by beating their chests. The flow of tears is not gendered, both men and women weep freely; but self-flagellation is an exclusive symbol of the male commemorative act. Ritual acts of blood – *tatbir* (cutting the flesh on one's forehead) and *janjeer jani* (slashing one's chest with chain/blade) – mark a strict gendered segregation and orient the public forms of ritual along the male gender.

Muharram processions, as a symbol of rebellion, emerged during the 1978–79 Iranian Revolution and culminated in the identification of Husayn's martyrdom as the ethical moral code of Shia men during the Iraq-Iran war (1980–1988). Husayn's martyrdom offered an efficacious tool to turn the Muharram paradigm from a ritual of mourning to a ritual of rebellion against oppressor Sunni Iraq (Hegland, 1983; Chelkowski, 2000). Since the 1990s, scholars, with particular focus on women's *majlis* (mourning ritual), noticed and discussed at length how the participation of women in the Muharram rituals exposed contradictions in social roles and ritual actions (Hegland, 1983; Kamran Scot Aghie, 2005). But, what one can observe is that neither did the rebellious martyr Imam always function as the template for individual Shia men, nor did Muharram commemoration succeed as the symbol of political counter-narrative when it was about the Karbala-centric emotion in the Indian sub-continent. In the Indian scenario, intercessory piety and pain for Imam Husayn act as the meditative medium to attain transcendence. Becoming his "true people" remains the aim of those performing the commemorative rituals.

Majlis is a strictly gender-segregated ritual. In the public ritual, the fact of men taking on the grieving voices of the women of *ahlul bayt* does not change the masculine thrust of the event. At the same time, grieving and surrender to pain in female poetic voice endow the masculine order another gender interpretation.

Simultaneously, the figure of Hazrat Abbas, the half-brother of Husayn, has emerged along with *ahlul bayt* both inside the elegies and as a symbol in the commemorative ritual. Abbas is eulogized for serving *ahlul bayt* and being martyred for his servitude in the battle of Karbala. By following the ethical moral codes offered by Imam Abbas, Shia men surrender to the greater pain and take the vow to offer servitude to the family of the Prophet. This discussion on gender and Shia religiosity suggests gender segregation, played out in the binary between blood and tears, the public display of self-flagellating male prowess and the private wailing of women. However, these may not be understood as gendered compartments in the normative patriarchal sense. Even in the identification with Abbas, an active-passive gender formulation between servitude (men) and surrender (women) cannot be demarcated. Rather, the Shia male public sphere needs women's active participation and moral self-disciplining to consolidate the community identity and piety.

While Shia women do not take active part in any public ritual, how such liminal ritual moves to and fro the imambaras ensures they occupy city streets and public transport. They also manoeuvre the largely Hindu urban landscape or Sunni ghetto with their veiled presence and forms of mourning. Their mobility through the non-sacred space carries the thrust of their aim and destination. The transcendence of piety and the action around the sacred sites integrally connects to the experiences of the trivial everyday life. The absence of a male community member during their public mobility or private mourning endows them with the authority to commute on their own and assemble, organise, manage, and sustain their own sacred site and performance. As collective gendered action or an individual woman's engagement with a collective, such performances are otherwise uncommon in their everyday living, especially when men have the ultimate say in the households that women manage. Subordination to religious norm here offers various ways for the women who inhabit the norms to develop their ethical moral will as religious subjects (Mahmood, 2011).[4] And according to the varied social af-filiations and positions of women, differences in exposure and needs multiply through the women's multiple ways of acting upon the sacred site. Even in and around the ritual actions, women create various layers to open up pos-sibilities of various interpretations of a singular space.

Women around Ripon Street generally visit two imambaras, Bibi Anaro and Haji Lane imambara. They also attend *majlis*es in a few 'house-imambaras,' which they call numbers 11 and 12 according to their street address. In the two small rooms and veranda of Haji Lane imambara that are made exclusively for women, their devotional frenzy reaches its zenith. Their chest-beating is rigorous and reverberates unlike at Bibi Anaro which has an exceptionally big hall allotted to women on the first floor. Farhat, a girl in her early 20s, reflects, "As in Haji Lane imambara, it's the women who do everything from cleaning the courtyard to informing the trustee about infrastructure maintenance. Their whole attitude changes after coming here." Her friend, Nusrat, added, "Also, when we are cramped in this small room, we feel we are doing everything together." "Also," Farhat added, "having no man around, women become their own persons." Women at Bibi Anaro imambara create impromptu groups without the *zakira*'s (female sermon giver) initiation. While the female *majlis* remains improvisational, the main sermon session takes place at the male quarters on the ground floor. Women are allowed to attend it, but by standing or sitting outside the hall. A *majlis* with a female sermon-giver has been a custom especially at private imambaras populated majorly with community members who are migrants from Uttar Pradesh with their Urdu-speaking lineage. At these private imambaras, women from the locality assemble to participate in the lament ritual. In those gatherings, the lament of the women flows seamlessly, catalyzed by the heart-rending oration of the Karbala battle by the *zakira*. The proceedings are intense yet serene and orchestrated inside a room in the house that holds all Muharram relics, including the small replica of Husayn's *rowza* (grave). The gendered nature of the house-*majlis*es is main-tained by scheduling them when male members are away at a *majlis* at Bibi Anaro. Kaukab Meerza is the family head of number 11. The Meerza family, which traces their lineage from Nawab Wajid Ali Shah, preserves Muharram relics carried here from their ancestral home, which had been a royal household in Lucknow. At this house, when I first started visiting imambaras, an elderly Hashmat Fatima (in her early 60s) delivered sermons and presided over the *majlis* at house-imambaras and Haji Lane imambaras.

Tucked away in some bylane near Ripon Street which continued to be marked as a "'minority bustee' (ghetto) in Calcutta Corporation maps till the 1950s, these households radiate an aura of authenticity and entitlement in the gathering of women with varied linguistic (Urdu and Hindi) affiliations, various class backgrounds and migration-settlement histories. In 2013, in one of such gatherings I met Manzilat Fatima in her mid-40s, who stood apart in her all-white attire, listening to the elegies without touching her chest or syncing her lips to the words unlike others. Manzilat, the eldest child of the house, had chosen a Sunni husband, and her children were also not a part of the Muharram commemoration. "But I make it a point to attend as many *majlis*es as I can. It is my own identity," Manzilat told me. "My children have not been brought up with this emotion."

Becoming Zaynab, becoming Abbas: The trans-local and multi-local turn

Translocal realization is the essence of a global Shia community with the site of Husayn's martyrdom lying beyond their local-national territories. Shias in West Bengal, with multiple imambaras strewn all over the Kolkata quarters and in the districts, have their locally fixed centres of Shia devotionalism. For the Kolkata Shias, it has always been the Shibtainabad Imambara in Metiabruz consecrated by Wajid Ali Shah as the replica of Bara Imambara in Lucknow. In this imambara, however, there is no tradition of women performing lamentations.

Shia men near Ripon Street always visited the Metiabruz imambara for the majlis there for that connects them with the imagined community spread across different quarters of Kolkata. But once the renovation of Bibi Anaro imambara started in 2011, men got interested in this local sacred site. Women also were excited after getting a separate entrance for the upper storey allotted specially for their congregation.

As explained earlier, the translocal is deeply embedded in the Shia imagination. The local Shia communities have always been connected with the dynamic translocal flow of religious and visual materials. Proliferation of art from Iran during and post Iran-Iraq war celebrating the ethos of Karbala and ethics of martyrdom and subsequent reproductions solidified the contours of visual piety for the community. As such receptions expanded the horizon of the imagined community. The impact of new media in the form of reception of the CDs and DVDs of *marsiya/nawha* transformed the community into a digital collective with new capacities of listening/viewing and participating in the religious discourses. The use of the web and social media is a recent phenomenon for the community. So far, it is also male dominated, with only a few female users. But what is perhaps important to notice here is how online religion gets intertwined with offline activities and how such male patterns of consumption and interpretation of multi-local religious elements organize both the public and private forms of devotion performed by the community men and women.

Since 2011, after Bibi Anaro imambara was renovated, it transformed from a humble one-storey house into a huge two-storey building, giving women a separate floor for their ritual mourning. But in the huge space of ritual performance, with its vast and open windows, the collective lament seems to dissipate in the air. Also, without any *zakira* to initiate the lament session, ritual actions do not have a well-knit structure like in the Haji Lane or house imambaras. Women finish off their session and rush down to wait on the stairs or in front of the closed door of the ground floor hall where the *zakir* – male sermon giver – sits on a *mimbar* (pedestal) and initiates the male audience into an elegy recitation and a *sineh-jani*. Once the *majlis* is over, women are allowed to enter the hall to circle around Imam Husayn's *rowza*. Such spatial segregation and formalization of male *majlis*es, as I understood from my repeated visits to this imambara from 2011 onwards, are still a matter of pride for women of the locality who come to attend the *majlis*. The newly invigorated interest to Bibi Anaro imambara, in a way, has lessened the emotional pull to Metiabruz for its *majlis*es and reaffirmed the position of Bibi Anaro in another multi-local network.

The architecture of Bibi Anaro has been developed by emulating Shia shrines in Iran and Iraq. The original references come from multi-local sources as sacred sites in UP, especially those in Lucknow, enter the digital visual imagination and proliferate on social media. As the façades of Bibi Anaro attempt to replicate the arches of prolific Lucknow imambaras, its courtyard simply and specifically mirrors the courtyard of Dargah Hazrat Abbas Alamdar in Rustom Nagar, Lucknow. A rectangular water tank, as a reminder of the thirsty beloved martyrs of Karbala, and a replica of Abbas' leather water bag were consecrated in the Bibi Anaro courtyard.

On the whole, with the advent of new media, the male ethical principle based on servitude became more structured by reclaiming an ethical template offered by Abbas. But what is interesting to notice is that despite the symbolic organization of the sacred site, the choice of elegies on Abbas, the growing use of red flags with Abbas' name painted/stitched on them to orient the male *Ashura* ritual along the figure of Abbas, the men's reading of the elegies considered to be Zaynab's speech, has not lessened by any means. In the *Ashura* processions of Kolkata, the most prominent form of servitude is performed when men carry the replica of the *alam* (flag/standard) that Abbas carried in the battle of Karbala. At the same time, such emulation of Abbas' moral template through identification does not mean a normative male orientation of the ritual as Zaynab and Sakina have remained two very important figures in the landscape of piety.

Atif Ali Khan, a young *nawhakhan* (elegy reader) in his early 20s, who becomes a bearer of Abbas' standard in the *Ashura* procession, earnestly explains the coexistence of Abbas and Zaynab. "There can't be any gender-wise division of the relevance of these two figures – Maula Abbas and Bibi Zaynab. They have two different causes and contexts. It is never like this that men specifically read Abbas and women Zaynab. Both are the core symbols of the community. Maula Abbas stands as the protector of *ahlul bayt* before he was killed in the battlefield of Karbala and BibiZaynab becomes the spokesperson for the community after the battle when Imam Husayn's son Zaynul Abedin, the fourth Imam, was too young for leadership. Then, it was Bibi Zaynab who united the Shia community."[5] Zaynab portrays a form of womanhood that strengthens the community, men and women alike.

When there was an extension of Bibi Anaro imambara with a separate entrance for women and a separate hall for prayer, it was much more than the patriarchal segregation of space. Such gendered segregation allowed women more access over a bigger sacred space where they act to transform the sacred place into space (Desplat, 2012). Pilgrimage, a sacred act open to the male members of the community alone when they visited the Metiabruz imambara, is now something that women have access to as well, as the esteem of Bibi Anaro as a site of communal congregation increases by the day. In the huge first floor hall, with open windows and Iranian pointed arches, women gather much before the *majlis*, an improvisational event depending on the gathering, and stay back well after the ritual is over.

As the male public performance creates a very specific local network of devotionalism reaffirming the connection between the Kolkata Shias and their co-religionists in Lucknow, a separate floor for women's majlis resonates with the Shrine of Zaynab in Syria which has had separate women's quarters after 2007 (Szanto, 2013:85). Popular history marks Abbas' *alam* (standard) with magical and healing powers. According to local history, it was discovered after an excavation in Lucknow and then consecrated in the courtyard of Dargah Hazrat Abbas. What is seen is a trans-national and multi-local forms of community network in transaction with the local gendered actions that interpret the sacred and the everyday function of the women. Such multi-local networking consolidates the authority of the Bibi Anaro imambara by enhancing the capacity of the community people and especially women in the local and competing sacred landscapes. Bibi Anaro imambara, which had been less influential compared to two others, (the Sibtainabad Imambara in Metiabruz and Golkothi Imambara near Chitpur, central Kolkata) now emerges as a new centre of Shia religiosity in the devotional landscape. Historically Bibi Anaro had always enabled women's ritual actions and its space unlike the older two imambaras which neither had any culture of women's *majlis* nor had created any scope for women to take part in any activity.

Online and offline Shia ritual: Old authorities, new authors

The newly emergent flood of online literacy and social media (especially Facebook) created a new belongingness to a dynamic imagined community online, enriched with multi-local experiences of trans-local Shia communities. While women in general are yet to become active online, the integral connection between online and offline activities by male users of social networking sites does change the women's contexts and modes of ritual participation at sacred sites. The transformation in the architectural structure of Bibi Anaro can be seen as a direct response to images found online and gradual exposure to ritual performances in various imambaras across regions posted on Facebook has made a direct impact on the way women act in the sacred space. As women's mourning rituals become dependent on the male *majlis* and meaningful only in the context of larger ritual functioning of the imambara as an institution, the open vast hall gives them scope to make this space habitable. In the sacred space, non-sacred acts like chatting, grouping, and even resting are performed as the frame of the *majlise*s. This open hall has become the only possible public (though gendered) space for Shia women in Kolkata to occupy as their own and extend the capacity of the ritual to their specific everyday experiences by engaging in class-wise or intra-class clusters outside of the ritual. As the external male domain weakens the power of women's ritual at the institutional level with more formal male private and public mourning sessions and commemorative performances, women's participation has grown more enthusiastic as they are unencumbered and in charge.

In the newly invigorated field of online literacy, Kamran Meerza, a man in his early 40s, has emerged an unlikely star, recording rituals and posting them on his Facebook account, sharing photographs of imambaras he has been visiting in north India and in different parts of West Bengal and creating an online archive for his Facebook friends. Through his Facebook account, various other trans-local and trans-national accounts can be connected as they remain enmeshed and ever-open.

Outside the realm of virtual importance, Kamran Meerza is an insurance agent who also happens to be the male descendent of the Wajid Ali Shah family that lives at the number 11 house. It has been an age-old tradition that the male procession of *Ashura* will go from Bibi Anaro imambara via the house of the royal family. But what has re-energised the position of this family is a growing awareness of and sensitivity to their Lucknow royal heritage which they themselves have become aware of recently. A lot of enterprises con-ducting heritage walks include Metiabruz. The lineage, which remained un-addressed in the public discourse till the recent past, has now become a part of their public identity and the family has started to respond to it in the religious and socio-political spheres. Kamran Meerza makes his unique position a social one by designating himself as a photographer on Facebook who brings the sacred to the secular, the transcendental to technology. His elder sister, food entrepreneur Manzilat, who has appeared in a previous section of this essay, has started her catering service that claims to revive Awadhi cuisine, au-thenticated by her connection to royalty. In her Facebook posts, she openly praises Priyanka Gandhi, granddaughter of late Congress Prime Minister Indira Gandhi, who will play a much bigger role in the 2019 general elections than in the past, by calling her 'The Tempest.' Her Facebook walls are also flooded with pictures of her new terrace eatery and eulogies for Begum Hazrat Mahal, her ancestor, the second wife of Wajid Ai Shah, who fought against the British during the Indian rebellion of 1887. She even sends blessings from Begum Hazrat Mahal to Priyanka Gandhi via her Facebook posts. Thus, recognition from the nation state by reclaiming a national patriotic identity has become a necessity for the Urdu-speaking elite Shia family in Kolkata, which is so evident in Manzilat's attempts to forge a connection between her ancestry and the Congress heiress in the name of nationalist belongingness.

There are other structural changes. Last year, when I visited the house of *zakira* Hushmat Fatima for a *majlis*, I was disappointed not to see the prolific *zakira* sitting on the makeshift pulpit of a chair covered in a black cloth.

This *zakira* in her narration of the episodes of the Karbala in her melodious, pensive and persuasive voice, was known to bring tears to the eyes of even her most prosaic listeners. Instead, the wife of Kamran Meerza, Nuzhat Zahrawas, was the *zakira* of that *majlis*. It was an achievement for Nuzhat, a woman in her early 30s, to come out of the private *majlis* cloister of her home imambara to become the *zakira* of her community. But I somehow felt she was not chosen to replace the previous *zakira* for her oratory, rather the newly invoked status of her family was the reason for her new post. Nuzhat's Facebook account says she is an MA in Urdu from the University of Calcutta. She has been chosen for the ring of authenticity, her marriage into a family with a royal lineage, and her degree in a language which needs to be hailed and reaffirmed as an identity-in-difference in a Bangla-Hindi speaking milieu. Manzilat's Facebook account eulogizes Urdu in her various posts, too. Both Kamran Meerza and Manzilat, the brother-sister duo, pointedly stress their origins from Lucknow, Uttar Pradesh, on Facebook. Such attempts invoke lineage, linguistic, and regional affiliations in a Bengali-speaking, Hindu-majority state by differentiating between Hindi-speaking Shia-Sunni migrants.

Conclusion

Can women consider themselves capable of 'acting' within given religious norms? Can 'doing' in the name of the divine be capacious enough to make a woman feel free, autonomous? From the ritual actions, can one general principle of 'gendered acting' be delineated? How does the interiority of sacred action that defines gender connect to the external societal forms that construct the Shia as a minority-within-minority community in India, especially a Bangla-speaking Hindu and Sunni Muslim context? The essay has addressed such questions by attempting an analysis of how Shia women engage with the sacred Shia ritual practices that might help their innovative doings in and around the ritual.

While 'innovative agency' of women (Hegland, 1983:256) in the religious space can be a productive tool to understand women as actors, that alone is insufficient to understand how Shia women consider gendered activity and capacity in a broader social context. Being religious and being economic actors are not antagonistic to the Shia women's everyday reality. The community's realization of its marginality and urge to go beyond that has resulted in education and jobs for its women. In this context, it will only be a truncated study if Shia women are taken up exclusively as a religious subject in the autonomous space of religion. But it also merits mention that their self-enhancement and social security come and will come as members of the Shia community, not as women alone.

Notes

1 Place-making capacities are observed by the scholars in a 'post-secular world' to understand their effects at varying spatial scales, with a special emphasis on contested identities and intercultural negotiations.

2 The Shias do not accept the Sunni caliphate and cultivate intercessory piety towards their Imams starting from Imam Ali.
3 Twelvers are the major sub-sect of the Shias who believe in the intercessory status of 12 imams from Ali to Mehdi.
4 Saba Mahmood intervenes in the secular feminist discourses on emancipation. But her exploration of the practices of pious Muslim women in Egypt leaves out the historicity and social functioning of those religious practices.
5 Personal correspondence with Atif Ali Khan on 20.02.2019.

References

Aghie, K. S. (2004). *The Martyrs of Karbala: Shia Symbols and Rituals in Modern Iran.* SeattlXCe: University of Washington Press.

Aghie, K S Ed. (2005). *The Women of Karbala: Ritual Performance and Symbolic Discourses in Modern Shi'i Islam.* Austin: University of Texas Press.

Alexander, C., Chatterjee, J. & Jalais, A. (2016). *The Bengal Diaspora: Rethinking Muslim Migration.* New York: Routledge.

Baumann, G. (1996). *Contesting Culture: Discourses of Identity in Multi-Ethnic London.* New York and Cambridge: Cambridge University Press.

Chatterjee, J. (2006). *The Spoils of Partition: Bengal and India, 1947-1967.* Cambridge: Cambridge University Press.

Chelkowski, P. & Dabashi, H. (2000). *Staging a Revolution: The Art of Persuasion in the Islamic Republic of Iran.* London: Booth-Clibborn Editions.

Desplat, P., Dorothea E., & Cole, J. R. I. (eds). (1988). Prayer in the City: The Making of Muslim Sacred Places and Urban Life (Bielefeld: Transcript, 2012). *Roots of North Indian Shi'ism in Iran and Iraq: Religion and State in Awadh, 1722-1859.* California: University of California Press.

Deeb, L. (2008). 'Exhibiting the "Just-Lived Past": Hizbullah's Nationalist Narrative in Transational Political Context'. *Comparative Studies in Society and History* 50, 2: 369–399.

D'Souza, D. (2014). *Partners of Zaynab: A Gendered Perspective of Shia Muslim Faith.* Columbia: University of South Carolina Press.

Flaskerud, I. (2010). *Visualizing Belief and Piety in Iranian Shi'ism.* New York: Continuum.

Hasan, Z. & Menon, R. (1991). *Unequal Citizens: A Study of Muslim Women in India.* New Delhi: Oxford University Press.

Hegland, M. (1983). "Ritual and Revolution in Iran." In Myron J. Aronoff (ed). *Political Anthropology Volume II; Culture and Political Change.* New Brunswick, NJ: Transaction Books.

Hyder, A. S. (2006). *Reliving Karbala: Martyrdom in South Asian Memory.* Delhi: Oxford University Press.

Khan, S. (2007). "Negotiating the *Mohalla*: Exclusion, Identity and Muslim Women in Mumbai," *Economic and Political Weekly* 42. Apr. 28 - May 4. 17: 1527–1533.

Mahmood, S. (2011). *Politics of Piety: The Islamic Revival and the Feminist Subject.* Princeton: Princeton University Press.

Mansouri, F., Lobo, M. & Johns, A. (2016). Grounding Religiosity in Urban Space: insights from multicultural Melbourne.*Australian Geographer* 47, 3: 295–310 http://dx.doi.org/10.1080/00049182.2016.1191134 accessed on 22.02.2019.

Rizvi, K. (2015). *The Transnational Mosque: Architecture and Historical Memory in the Contemporary Middle East.* Chapel Hill: The University of North Carolina Press.

Sachedina, A. A. (1994). A minority within a minority: The case of the Shi'a in North America. In Y. Y. Haddad and J. Idleman (ed.) *Muslim communities in North America.* New York: State University of New York Press.

Scharbrodt, Oliver. (2018). A minority within a minority?: The complexity and multilocality of transnational Twelver Shia networks in Britain. published online 8 November 2018 *Contemporary Islam* https://doi.org/10.1007/s11562-018-0431-0 accessed on 25.02.2019.

Szanto, E. (2013). "Beyond the Karbala Paradigm: Rethinking Revolution and Redemption in Twelver Shi'a Mourning Rituals." *Journal of Shi'a Islamic Studies VI.* 1:75–91.

Takim, L. (2009). *Shi'ism in America.* New York: New York University Press.

Part IV

Introduction to fundamentalist states of mind in the clinical space

Paula L. Ellman

The topic of the fundamentalist state of mind is a relevant focus in today's world where a populism trend has taken hold in all corners of the world. Minds have narrowed, priorities are focussed on one's own personal gains. Fundamentalism can be considered as an effort to strengthen one's grounding in an identity and experience of belonging can bring a sense of empowerment. The investment in certainty offers a refuge. The two papers in this section approach the topic of the fundamentalist state of mind in the clinical space in two very different ways. The first paper by Mallika Akbar is a presentation of a clinical case where the theme is on breaking the rules. The fundamentalist mind rigidly adheres to rules without allowing for space to think on one's own. In contrast to the fundamentalist mind, Dr. Akbar's patient lives a life of pursuing exceptions to rules that carry his wishes for omnipotence. The patient is always alone, left out, yearning to be on the inside, and ready to violate boundaries to get there. Dr. Akbar describes her patient's initial avoidance of bringing his desires into the transference, and then he brings her in as the voyeur, creating in the treatment the stimulating threesome that has always excited him. The threesome is exciting but is also dreaded as he is left feeling excluded. He yearns for the place of merger yet his wishes for the omnipotent solution make it impossible for him find satisfaction. The fantasied merger disavows aspects of separateness that is unbearable because of unmourned losses and the intolerance for bearing pain. The result is the patient's perverse solution where the patient's stimulating sexual pursuits become his way to feel alive in the midst of a frozenness in his internal emotional world. Dr. Akbar considers closely the transference countertransference as she is brought in as the voyeur, the position the patient, himself, often occupies. The projections of envy, of being the one left out, were experienced by the analyst. At the same time the patient's emptiness and deadness, the internalised maternal object, is likewise experienced countertransferentially. The patient's descriptions of his sexual involvements demonstrate his efforts to realise the fantasies of omnipotence and grandiose merger. He engages in the dance between feeling nothing and feeling too much as he seeks stimulation in sadoma-sochistic relationships where he has the overriding terror of feeling nothing, and believing that the object is out of his reach. In contrast to the funda-mentalist mind where exceptions are not tolerated, this patient lives with the belief that he needs warrant exception, granting him a place of grandiosity.

The patient cannot accept many fundamental truths – the but yet there is a fundamental impetus that motivates his perversion.

Dr. Dastur brings her psychoanalytic mind to examine the film DEVI by Satyajit Ray, a film about Devi, the all-embracing Mother Goddess wor-shipped in India in prehistoric times. Her consideration of the film is that it offers a depiction of the fundamentalist mind. It is a story of 100 years ago, a time when rural Indian women were under male domination. The wealthy patriarch and widower, Kalinkinkar, in his struggle with aging, his fear of death, his sexual desires, his wishes to merge with maternal object, his oedipal rivalry, and his envy of his married son has a dream that directs him to cast his son's wife, Doya, in the place of Devi the goddess. Dr. Dastur views Kalinkinkar's solution as his efforts to maintain his psychic equilibrium and become the child of omnipotent mother who protects from death. She states, "He infiltrates and colonizes the mind of the young woman," allowing for a delusional empowerment and preventing awareness of corporeal separateness for the object. The daughter-in-law counter-identifies with the projections and likely due to the rage at her husband's abandonment that Dr. Dastur suggests facilitates her participation in this folie a deux delusion. Religious devotion replaces lust. Differentiation is compromised. There is a loss of self as fantasy takes the place of symbolic thought. It appears to me that the psychic mechanisms that Dr. Dastur describes are the mechanisms that are character-istic of the fundamentalist state of mind. Projective identifications can at times become halluncinatory, and make for a disintegration of thinking and sym-bolic representation. For the fundamentalist, the object is experienced as omnipotent and attaching oneself to the object the subject can thereby share in the omnipotence.

While approached from two varying vantage points, these two papers be-come partners in the consideration of the fundamental mind and its attributes.

6 Peeping in through the keyhole

Mallika Akbar

The allusion to fundamentalist states of mind brings up for me notions of psychic rigidity, strict adherence to rules and dogmas, masking a high degree of omnipotence. The clinical case I present has antithetical characteristics: it is about violations, crossing boundaries, breaking rules. This too is omnipotent as it presumes an autonomous self which can breach limits with impunity. Wilfred Bion has spoken of how contact with reality can be masked by the operation of an omnipotent phantasy that is intended to destroy either reality or the awareness of it. Perversion is here understood as a distortion of reality and, by this reckoning, the transgressive and the fundamentalist are both perverse states of mind.

Since the time Freud (1905, 1931) saw perversion in all sexuality which was not heterosexual intercourse, psychoanalytic thinkers have sought to further our understanding of the perverse impetus. Perverse sexuality was described by Stoller (1974) as the conversion of infantile trauma into adult triumph, the defiance and victory over the internal controlling mother who threatens engulfment. Etchegoyen (1978) points out that the perverse patient is only in communication with his body through his intellect; he is aware of his instincts not as desire but as ideology; for the perverse patient, shut in the world of ideologies, the polemic is what is vital. Ogden (1996) says the perversity of the transference-countertransference derives from the patient's use of particular forms of sexualisation as a way of protecting against psychological deadness.

My presentation deals with a 45-year-old patient who has never really stepped out of his parents' bedroom. Nilesh is a respected academic who has creatively engaged with various political and social liberal causes. He travels widely for work and pleasure. Nevertheless, right from the beginning, he brought to the consulting room a self which seemed barely alive. He had panicked when he noticed that the trees and plants which he had always loved no longer moved him.

In one of his early sessions, Nilesh had laughed while saying he didn't really know why he had come for analysis. He was successful, had stable and loving relationships, many friends, and enough money ... but there were just a few things that were troubling him. He found he woke up crying every morning, there was an unpleasant tingling sensation in his genital region which he couldn't get rid of, he has had irritable bowel syndrome for several years, he has such a loving mother, and yet he is always snapping at her.... Some time later, he also spoke of feeling, deep within him, a hollowness and a void which made no sense to him. He tried to protect himself by taking refuge in the structure of BDSM (acronym for bondage and discipline, dominance and submission, sadism and masochism). It gave him an identity and clarity that he did not have otherwise. Nevertheless, there was something about the nature of his desiring self which came layered with pain and anxiety. He said he would rather die than lose his sexual desire, he worried about growing old, and being wrinkled and unattractive. What would happen to him when his mother died? What if, in spite of all the precautions he has taken, he had to manage life alone...?

Nilesh came for therapy nearly four years ago, utterly broken, as he had just learnt that his partner in the BDSM community was seeing other men and women. He said he was unhinged by what he called his "insane" bouts of jealousy and possessiveness. Nilesh has been in a long-term committed homosexual relationship with a partner who is not part of this community and who lives in another city. However, it has been his imaginative role-playing in the BDSM group as a submissive to dominant women, with all the attendant humiliations, intensities, and pain, which has excited and rejuvenated him and given him reprieve from a crippling deadness.

Nilesh had scant memories of his early life though he was quick to assert that there was nothing that had been traumatic then and which needed to be forgotten. As the youngest of three siblings and as the only son, he has felt special and cherished, especially by his beautiful mother. His parents were loving with each other and of their children; there was really nothing that was amiss. He was always on time for analysis, walking in with unhurried, mea-sured steps with just a brief glance in my direction. He spoke in a soft, low voice, there were no angry outbursts at all, and even the occasional tears flowed very quietly. His life seemed to roll along fairly smoothly and I was mostly left to wonder why he seemed so committed to therapy. What was the real reason? There had to be something ... something more ... but I had no idea. In retrospect, I understand this as being part of the problem he came with. The patient had a sense of pain but did not have the capacity to suffer it; he came for analysis with the hope that therapy would help him avoid bearing his pain.

He recalled more than once a memory of being awake as a child at night on a bed to the left of his parents' bed. Yet another recollection was of lying down between his aunt and uncle and of placing his uncle's hand on the aunt's breast when he thought they were both asleep. He was a grown teenager when he found himself obsessively looking at the breasts and crotches of random people. He was terrified he would be caught and shamed so he avoided as much interaction with others as he possibly could. As a young man and even until now, this patient has drawn a veil of secrecy around his sexual life. He has had several affairs with men and women but for his family and especially for his mother, he has needed to be the sexually naive, adoring son she has always loved. He could only love and desire in hiding, as if he was always in touch with a jealous, disapproving object. From the time he was 20 years old he has lived away from the parental home. Away but not quite away as he has managed to find families to live with. It's always been a family of three: a couple, whether homosexual or heterosexual, and Nilesh in the spare bedroom. It has been important for him to never share this intimate space with his own partner; always just the couple and him.

This family configuration was also present in the internal home he psychically lived in. Here too, a couple is always present, engaged with each other, and he is close by, watching, occupying a vantage point outside the pair. His gaze is fixed on the phantasised interaction between the other two, not necessarily father and mother, and it was only in the looking that he was aroused and excited. In the consulting room, I felt I was being kept out of his mind and the precious space the patient and his objects occupied. I felt useless, cold and frigid, a container for his non-desiring self. While he owned his vitality and sexual energy in the phantasised threesome, the space he occupied with me was polite and sparse; no real feelings entered this arid desert. We were an uncreative couple paradoxically bound together by some yet unknown neediness.

A dream he brought in the second year significantly changed the tenor in the room. Very briefly, he dreamt that he was having exciting intercourse with his mother while his father was quietly watching them from a window opening into the room. I ventured to suggest that it was perhaps I at the window and that he wanted me to watch him having sex with a collated mother-father object. He received this with a non-committal "that's interesting." However, he seemed excited to be in a different role in the dream. He knew his own perverse desire to be participating while watching the phantasised intercourse. That his voyeuristic desires could be safely deposited in me was a new experience for him. I realised that it was not just projection and projective identification here; in the countertransference, my own perverse desire to enter his world and participate as the looker-on had been tapped. Though in the transference he kept me at a distance and never acknowledged any feelings linked with me, I found myself wanting to get closer, to penetrate a space which had contours which we had not seen before. In my perverse countertransference, I was now part of his BDSM world. I was his sexually dead internal object whom he had seduced and aroused with his sexual excitement. Under his omnipotent control, I was also looking in aggressively, stripping the couple of privacy and potency. In our secret, underground world, everything felt exciting and alive. It took me a long while to recognize the perverse scenario we had together created as an escape from our emptiness.

The BDSM was an escape from what was in fact real: intolerable feelings of numbness, deadness, and loneliness. It also put Nilesh in touch with unacknowledged feelings of rage, envy, and jealousy. In the consulting room, what slowly emerged was a cherished phantasy of a womb-like space in which the patient lay in a foetal position, hand on shoulder, occasionally peeping out but not coming out at all. "It's just me and what I want … I feel safe … I like the boundaries … the sense of not being invaded … of being all curled up." He described this state as spiritual bliss, only the moon and trees, bypassing human beings. It was an escape from the internal home he inhabited, the home with the couple and him; sometimes happy and sometimes torturing him with the sense of being excluded and very alone. "I am not safe in or out, its so bad … I hate this infant," he once said … "it makes me clingy, it is exhausting and it hinders my spiritual journey." Occasionally, we got in touch with an anxious and frightened person, exuding a longing to be held closely. It is paradoxical that, however many relationships he had, the closeness was never enough.

Freud has postulated a connection between post-natal thought and emotional life, and pre-natal life. While imagining the mind of the foetus, he said, "There is much more continuity between intra-uterine life and earliest infancy than the impressive caesura of the act of birth allows us to believe." In "Caesura" written in 1977, Wilfred Bion took this connection even deeper. Bion contended that birth was a pause, not a rupture, in the continuing business of life. He added, "Events in the womb of time eventually show themselves in the conscious life of the person concerned who then has to act in the situation which has now become real." Bion here is predicating the foetal mind, full of unmentalised experiences, which inevitably finds expression in our conscious selves.

Much of what Nilesh brought to the consulting room and my own emotional responses to it allows us to conceive of a psychological birth which has been painful, linked with a tearing apart, a searing loss, with noises that were too loud and lights that were too bright, as if early illusions of safety and oneness were suddenly shattered, long before he was ready. Many of his associations were about wanting to merge with the lover, about searching for the oceanic experience of oneness, of being held tightly from the back by strong arms. "That's the real thing … this room is the womb I am looking for.… I don't want to get out of here.…" His need was to hold on to a safe, contoured, and boundaried space which would allow him to feel again the bliss he believed he once knew. It was also about denying the truth of separateness. Suzanne Maiello in 1995 hypothesised that the sound of the mother's voice, alternating with silence, may give the foetus a proto-experience of both presence and absence. This pre-natal proto-object, which she called the "sound object," establishes the foetus's awareness of separateness, of an object who can be present as well as absent. Nilesh was unable to mourn the first separation, that from his mother, and this was the precursor to other unmourned separations, other unmourned losses. The overarching need was to deny any feeling that might raise possibilities of suffering.

The ways in which the patient negotiated the complexities of the Oedipal situation reveal a fuller picture of his perverse internal world. In "The Missing Link" (1989), Ronald Britton has described the primal family triangle: the child with two links connecting him separately with each parent and the same child being confronted by the link between them which excludes him. In a bid to deny the threatened exclusion, this patient was locked in an internal threesome, just the couple and him. When in phantasy he is with the couple, he is right inside the couple, fully participating in all that the couple does. When outside the couple but inside the threesome, he bypasses the pain of being excluded. His jealousy and rage are disavowed, unseen in locked compartments within him. Here there is no fear, nothing to be agitated about, his aloneness and inner deadness simply denied. But this was also a falsehood. For Nilesh, truly and fully recognising parental sexuality and the fact that they had a relationship with each other was catastrophic; being mentally always present with them was exciting and has allowed him to evade his envy of the couple. Perversely, his presence was also a way of preventing parental intercourse. He once categorically said, "I'm just not okay looking at beauty, at Nature … I completely relate it to my parents having sex … having sex in the same room. … I can't look … it's beautiful … I'm there but I'm not there…." He struggled with his gaze drawn to the object and wanting to look away as well. Both desires were intensely felt, leaving him in a wobbly emotional state. I saw the sexualisation as his way of feeling alive. He needed to bypass pain, and for this Nilesh had deadened his capacity to feel. The hypersexualisation was his way of rousing himself to increasingly sporadic feelings of aliveness.

Melanie Klein has spoken of the child's fascination for and terror of the combined object, of parents united in an everlasting sexual embrace, a phantasy of the mother containing the father's penis or the whole father and the father incorporating the mother's breast and genitals. Nilesh's phantasies of the couple having sex made him envious and fearful. But if he wasn't right there with the internal couple, he felt discarded and ugly. In the consulting room, jealous and despairing tears would flow abundantly if he learnt that his partner was attracted to someone else. So much activity in his external life was about calming himself, to quieten the persecutory tumult within. He tried to bypass the anxiety of being left out by seeking daily, hourly phone contact with his lover, much like permanent intercourse, not allowing space for any rival. He constantly felt, however, the precariousness of walking on thin ice, a crack could plunge him into terrifying dark waters. The rumble from the mix of desire, fear, guilt, and conflict was a constant internal presence.

He triumphed over the internal couple by making me the excited observer in the room, witness to his many dyadic relationships. By doing so, Nilesh was taking care of several psychic needs: he was projecting into me that split-off part of him which was excited and desiring to be part of the parental intercourse; with me as the observer, he didn't have to feel left out or choose one or the other parent: he was keeping both. I was the internal mother who was so quiet, untouched, and two-dimensional, almost dead, whom he needed to arouse; in the transference, he was not the one with envy and longing, he was the envied one. I also felt he needed me to really know what he has truly felt all along despite all the psychical manoeuvring: alone, excluded, not knowing what to do with his desiring self.

In spite of the chaos and unhappiness, he was unable to relinquish his sexual claim on his internal parents. He was very sad one day when he said, "I can feel it in my blood .... I have no memory ... no desire for my parents ... yet I know that's it. ... so vague and yet not vague ... it's hazy ... not hazy ... it's in my body ... so strange." The internalised couple was primarily a sexual couple, its other attributes were barely acknowledged. In his external life, he chose as partner an accomplished man whose feminine traits made him especially desirable. Nilesh is the child in the relationship, he feels emotionally held and taken care of and he has spoken of them growing old together. But there is hardly any sex, or it is boring "vanilla" or conventional sex. It was as if his loved and loving object could not be his sexual object. He was attached to the internal combined sexual object and it has seemed that he is always searching for it in his external world. His foray into the BDSM world – without telling his partner of course – was a way of filling the internal gap, of reassuring himself that he could have it all, even if from different sources. This community of people with similar disappointments and similar longings, its strict code of conduct, its rules and strictures offered possibilities of re-discovering the boundaried internal space with all the magic it promised. He got sexually involved with a beautiful married woman willing to play out their shared sexual phantasies.

He was now in touch, excessively again, with parts of him that he had kept in darkness for so long. In his "play" appointments, he was the child being held in a close, sexual embrace by a strong mother; at another, he was the tender mother feeding his adoring child at his bounteous breasts; at yet an-other, he got pleasure in being physically hurt and sexually humiliated by a powerful woman. His masochistic need was to feel that his body was identified with the mother's body with whom he then fused. In play, his phantasy of the fused self submitting to a sadistic father was enacted, providing both perverse gratification and bypassing his dreaded phantasy of parents in union. As Janine Chasseguet-Smirgel has said, "the genital penis is swept away, transformed into a whip ... undergoing a strange metamorphosis; this metamorphosis ... contributes to pleasure, a mix of sexual pleasure and narcissistic triumph."

It sometimes seemed to me that his "play" in the BDSM group was imbued with more feeling and reality than the life he led overground. But the "play" followed strict rules and there were limits. He brought to the consulting room a sense of weariness, as if he was caught and could not escape the dancing movement between feeling nothing and feeling too much. He was trapped by his desire for excess in order to feel something real and emotional. His deepest fear was of not feeling anything at all, of not being able to smell the flowers, of being dead while alive. It terrified him to see that these unfeeling states could be mitigated only with that intense sense of too muchness, as in the BDSM.

His fears kept him in a difficult-to-describe state of pain. He spoke of feeling held and then being dropped, of knowing the security of loving arms and the terror of falling from those arms. His unmet wish was to be "somebody's priority in a non-dutybound way." In "Attention and Interpretation" written in 1970, Bion speaks of "people who are so intolerant of pain or frustration that they feel the pain but will not suffer it and so cannot be said to discover it...." My countertransferential experience was of holding an infant who struggled against being born, who has subsequently felt through his adult life the raw pain of emerging into a new state of mind. It was not just about being born, it was also about being torn out, being held and not held, about feeling the loss of connection in every inch of his being. The realisation that separation would happen, that he would be longing once again for the same object, filled him with despair. It seemed that however close the object was, it was always out of reach.

What might be the internal configurations which have made Nilesh the way he is? We posit a sense of an internalised family which did not make room for or tolerate real and authentic feelings like jealousy and desire. Everything needed to be in order on the surface, if disquiet or fear were experienced, they had to be brushed aside or buried; it was important not to disturb the preferred self-image. We see a family so fused together that it was unable to provide the protective emotional cover that the child needs. Frances Tustin has pointed out that it is within the healthy sheltering of the post-natal womb that psychological integrations take place. Having a mother who can patiently hold and contain her child's terror, rage, and longing is by far the best chance a child has for developing the capacity for basic trust. This patient sensed his mother as one who loved him but loved too much, a mother who used him autistically, as a part of herself. He struggled with feeling stifled by the object's possessiveness, yet knowing that the only way to keep his mother – and himself – alive was by fusing with her and denying her separateness.

He was left with a tenuous and anxious hold on what was real. In his internal world, the male and female parts were not integrated, entangling him in a web of uncertainty. He couldn't choose a partner without soon desiring another, and then back again, stuck in a blurred space with no ground on which to place his feet. A morbid fear of gaps, of ruptured links, was evident in the meticulous planning that went into every aspect of his life. Nothing could be left to chance. One day, he lost his way to my consulting room. He eventually arrived, hugely distraught. He said, "I kept typing in your address and the gps kept taking me to another block. ... I was going round and round in circles, I was lost. I didn't know where I was anymore ... it was so scary." I was listening to someone who was wandering, alone, and lost in an internal world which was threatening and anchorless. I had become the elusive object whose sheltering mind could not be reached.

Nilesh negotiated the labyrinthine path to adulthood by evading certain truths, by fostering other half-truths, by creating boxes in his psyche to separate intimate relationships and to not allow access to others. In the course of our shared journey, I have experienced him as being trapped in the constant oscillation between feeling nothing and feeling excessively, an existence which was neither here nor there, neither inside the womb nor outside it, neither male nor female, neither homosexual nor heterosexual, neither dead nor alive.

This fuzzy space was also his preferred space; it felt safe and allowed him to omnipotently believe that he could have it all, that he did not have to choose. Though he was in pain constantly, it was an amorphous pain, allowing him to vainly hope that it could somehow be bypassed.

But he has come for analysis because there is also a part of him which is tired of living anxiously in an uncertain world. Bion called it the truth drive, pointing out that a hatred of truth leads to a hatred of life itself. Nilesh's political and social beliefs allowed him to conceal even from himself what he knew to be true psychically. His polemics rubbished marriage and monogamy; polyamory was celebrated, patriarchy and boundaries of any kind were uncool. So he too was shocked when he discovered in our work that his search for more and more excitement was taking him nowhere really, that sexual rivals threw him into sleepless rages, that his erotic years were over and that all he really really wanted was to be in a monogamous relationship with a loving woman. It was a painful truth to take in, it completely negates the trajectory he had envisioned for himself and he is aware that he has only partially accepted this part of him.

Conclusion

It has been difficult for the patient, as it is for many of us, to accept what Roger Money-Kyrle called the "facts of life": first, the difference between generations, second, the difference between the sexes, and third, the reality of the passage of time. Nilesh has sought to evade certain other truths as well: that he is born from parental intercourse and that he is not part of that dyad, that he can't return to the womb, that he is not fused with his mother, that he is separate, that he is not a child, that play is only play and that he still has to return to the real world, that he has no choice but to suffer the pain that these truths entail.

The maze he found for himself to deny reality pushed him into a perverse relationship with me and with reality itself. It also alienated him from himself. Nilesh has deadened himself in order not to feel pain and, in the process, he has lost the capacity to feel emotions. This deadness makes him absent to the varied experiences that life entails, and he is more than dimly aware of this. BDSM is then a last-ditch, desperate effort to feel. It is more about searching for exciting sensations than it is about sexual desire, intimacy, or connectedness. "Perversion creates a frozen ritual that dissociates the perverse subject from his own vitality rather than expressing uniqueness " (Dana Amir, 2013). A life journey which began as a revolt against a fundamentalist state of mind, with the anarchic throwing out of all rules of life, has become a rigid, omnipotent, and ultimately stultifying attempt to deny the emptiness inside.

Am most grateful to Avner Bergstein and to Nilofer Kaul for the brainstorming and the insights.

References

Alvarez, A. (2012). *The Thinking Heart*. London: Routledge.

Amir, D. (2013). The Chameleon Language of Perversion. *Psychoanal. Dial.*, 23(4):393–407.

Bergstein, A. (2013). Transcending the Caesura: Reverie, Dreaming and Counter-Dreaming. *Int. J. Psycho-Anal.*, 94:621–644.

Bion, W.R. (1959). *Attacks on Linking*. In *Second Thoughts: Selected Papers on Psychoanalysis*. London: Heinemann.

Bion, W.R. (1962). *Learning From Experience*. London: Heinemann.

Bion, W.R. (1977). *Caesura*. In *Two Papers: The Grid and Caesura*. London: Karnac.

Britton, R. (1989). Chapter Two: The Missing Link: Parental Sexuality in the Oedipus Complex. *The Oedipus Complex Today, Clinical Implications*. London: Karnac.

Britton, R., Feldman, M., O'Shaughnessy, E. (1989). *The Oedipus Complex Today: Clinical Implications*. London: Karnac.

Chasseguet-Smirgel, J. (1991). Sadomasochism in the Perversions: Some thoughts on the destruction of reality. *J. Amer. Psychoanal. Assoc.*, 39:399–415.

Emanuel, R. (2001). A-Void: An Exploration of Defences against Sensing Nothingness. *Int. J. Psychoanal.*, 82(6):1069–1084.

Etchegoyen, R. H. (1978). Some Thoughts on Transference Perversion. *Intl. J. Psychoanal.*, 59:45–53.

Feldman, M., Spillius, E.B. (Editors) (1989). *Psychic Equilibrium and Psychic Change: Selected Papers of Betty Joseph*. London: Routledge.

Freud, S. (1905). Three Essays on the theory of Sexuality. *Standard Edition*, Vol. 7. London: Hogarth Press.

Freud, S. (1919). A Child Is Being Beaten: A Contribution to the Study of the Origin of Sexual Perversions. *Standard Edition*, Vol. 17. pp. 179–204.

Freud, S. (1931). Female Sexuality. *Standard Edition*, Vol. 21. London: Hogarth Press.

Giovacchini, P.L. (1989). *Countertransference: Triumphs and Catastrophes*. New York, Jason Aronson.

Grotstein, J.S. (2007). *A Beam of Intense Darkness: Wilfred Bion's Legacy to Psychoanalysis*. London: Karnac.

Joseph, B. (1971). A Clinical Contribution to the Analysis of a Perversion. *Int. J. Psychoanal.*, 52:441–449.

Khan, M.M.R. (1979). *Alienation in Perversions*. London: Hogarth Press

Maiello, S. (1995). The Sound Object: A Hypothesis about Prenatal Auditory Experience And Memory. *J. Child Psychother.*, 21:23–41.

Ogden, T.H. (1996). The Perverse Subject of Analysis. *J. Amer. Psychoanal. Assoc.*, 44:1121–1146.

Segal, H. (1975). *Introduction to the Work of Melanie Klein*. London: Hogarth Press.

Spillius, E.B. (Editor) (1988) *Melanie Klein Today*. Vol. 2. London: Routledge.

Stein,R. (2005). Why Perversion?: 'False Love' and the Perverse Pact. *Int. J. Psycho-Anal.*, 86:775–799.

Steiner, J. (2004). *Containment, Enactment, and Communication*. In *In pursuit of Psychic Change: the Betty Joseph Workshop*. London: Brunner-Routledge.

Stern, D. (1985). *The Interpersonal World of the Infant*. New York: Basic Books.

Stoller, R.J. (1974). Hostility and Mystery in Perversion. *Ann. Psychoanal.*, 2:197–212.

Tustin, F. (1983). Thoughts on Autism with Special Reference to a Paper by Melanie Klein. *J. Child Psychother.*, 9(2).

Tustin, F. (2016). Autistic Processes. J. *Child Psychother.*, 42(1).

7 An analysis of the film DEVI by Satyajit Ray: The colonisation and scotomisation of a mind

Minnie K. Dastur

The story of Devi took place a 100 years ago. Sadly, however the story still happens in many pockets of India, where women are still under the domination of male oriented traditions. The movie faced a lot of protests from religious fundamentalists because of its decrying of superstition and the damage and harm it can cause. However, it went on to receive the President's Silver medal and was nominated for the Palm d'Or at the Cannes Film Festival. Each frame in the film is a masterpiece in itself and serves two narrations: the external story and the parallel internal psychic story. It shows the tragedy of uncontrolled superstition and the devastating effects of projective identification; how a mind that has not been securely integrated, a sense of 'Skin Ego' not formed, can be colonised, and scotomised in the service of a narcissistic alliance. It Illustrates the making of a Second Skin, under the guise of religious devotion and worship, the creation of a False Self. The film is set in rural Bengal and tells the story of an ageing, widowed patriarch, Kalikinkar's devotion to the goddess (Devi) Durga; his oedipal conflict with his young and successful son, his hidden unconscious lust/love for the beautiful daughter-in-law, Doya. He then has a dream which he believes is a revelation that the goddess has come down to earth in the form of his daughter-in-law. He sets her up, apart, in a sanctified room to be worshipped. This whole process comes apart and destroys the life of all involved in it.

The opening credits are like a Prelude to a Symphony. The music takes us through the emotional impact that will be created and repeated along with the relevant scenes. The visuals start with the white plaster cast face of Durga. Durga is the powerful, yet more benevolent and compassionate mother goddess (Ma). Kali is the alter Ego of Durga, significantly, from whose forehead she has sprung. She is depicted in a very frightening demonic way and is the personification of death, destruction, and the power of black magic. The goddess has a third eye in the centre of her forehead. This Inner Eye refers to the eye that provides perception beyond ordinary sight. The plaster cast has the outlines; the slant of the large eyes, the mouth that has a sort of mysterious smile that could be benign and cruel at the same time. The accompanying music starts with a foreboding air, slowly turning melancholic. The plaster cast now gets more and more embellished with assorted ornaments and the music turns frenzied. It is the blank face of Doya on which her story will be written. It also represents Kalinkinkar's supposed credulous and protector self, hiding the cruelty that he is going to perpetrate. It foreshadows the DREAM that is to come and is the fulcrum to the story. It plays the same role in the film as the Wolf Man's dream plays in "The History of an Infantile Neurosis" and is just as masterfully shown.

The protagonist is Kalikinkar, a widowed worshipper of Durga, the wealthy, ageing patriarch living in his huge mansion still with absolute control over all. He has two sons. Umaprasad, the younger son, is a bright, intellectual studying in English in Calcutta. Doya, his beautiful, meek, and young wife, is not so educated, and is left behind to look after the father-in-law and the home. As a traditional daughter-in-law, she dutifully tends to old Kalikinkar. She is shown bringing him his tea, giving him his medicines, massaging his feet, etc. The elder son Taraprasad, helpless under the domination of his father, has resorted to alcoholism. His wife Harasundari, is not so meek and sub-missive. They have a young boy child, Khoka, who is encouraged by Doya, is very attached to her, as she is to him.

The names of the two main characters deeply involved in the unfolding of this tragedy are both related to the goddess Kali. Kalikinkar, the dreamer of the dream, meaning devotee or servant of Kali. Doya meaning mercy is the compassionate aspect of the Goddess. She is the hapless victim that makes his 'dream come true.' On the other hand we can also question this, because "it takes two to tango." The Goddess as a loving mother goddess who can destroy death as well as demons, is significant for Kalikinkar's worship of her, to control his internal demons, his hidden sexual desire for the young Doya, his rivalry with his son, his fear of his inevitable death, and his longing to merge with his mother. It is about a self still fused with the primal object, a separation that has never truly come about and been mourned. The dis-placement of censored drives into the worship of the Mother Goddess and thereafter projected into Doya, making her into a goddess. She is thereby in his control, no longer available to his son, and he can still disguise all this envy and destruction under the religious façade. Both from the outside, as well as inside, within himself.

Devi is not only about superstitious worship, but broadens the fold to show how it is used to serve hidden conscious and unconscious wishes and phantasies. It is about an old man's struggle with his ageing, his intense narcissism, his strong oedipal rivalry, and envy; the use of hallucination as a defence mechanism to maintain psychic equilibrium; and about the power of splitting, projective identifications, faulty mirroring, attacks on linking, ego disintegration, and the failure of the capacity to think. There is adhesive identification on both sides. When you are attached to someone or some powerful organisation, adhesive identification gives you a false sense of power. "The individual related through adhesiveness (in autistic phenom-enon), in which he adheres to contiguous surfaces, thereby avoiding any space ... thus preventing intolerable awareness of corporeal separation from the object.... This would be an autistic protective manoeuvre which leads the individual to relate to the object by adhesive identification" (Korbivcher, 2013: 649). This holds true for Kalikinkar with his Durga worship but also for Doya, who has not had the potential space to find herself. She is straightjacketed into the traditional submissive role of wife, daughter-in-law, mother, but not herself. Her frustration and anger cannot be expressed if she is to be 'good,' loved, and respected. Kalikinkar can thus infiltrate and colonise her body and mind (but somewhere it is a willing mind) in an omnipotent and intrusive way, producing a form of narcissistic and adhesive identification, at the cost of alienation from her own true identity.

These kinds of projective mechanisms create a scotoma, a blind spot, which blurs both Doya's and Kalikinkar's capacity to see what is happening in that very space that is being blanked out. The psychosis of both is based on the Pleasure Principle at the avoidance of the Reality Principle, be it pleasure in love and acquisition, or pleasure in hatred, revenge, and destruction. They, cannot therefore 'think' in the Bionian sense and are in a swirl of Beta elements – symbolic equations – that are only useful for evacuation. This leads to a disintegration of the very function of 'thinking' and symbolic representation, that can hold the ego together, the hate and the love, the compassion and the aggression. For Kalikinkar, there are active attacks on linking. For Doya, it seems more as if her links were never strong enough – there is a "deficit/defect in the capacity to link" (Alvarez, 1998) and thus the capacity to know and recognize oneself and thoughts.

The film begins with a large procession that takes the idol of Durga, on a highly decorated frame, to the river for immersion. This is the culmination of nine days of worship – Durga Puja. The front of the framework on which the goddess is placed is much decorated, but we get a view of it from behind as it is being carried out for the final immersion into the river. We see it for what it is, after the idol is removed; just a makeshift bamboo, wooden, lifeless frame. Next we see a sacrifice being made to the goddess. The idolator holds the sword high, before it comes down on the hapless victim. Then, instead of the gruesome spurt of blood, we see the explosions of the fireworks. This is the fate of Doya; worshipped, adorned, only to be sacrificed to Kalikinkar's explosive projective identifications. The explosion represents the minute fragmentation of Kalikinkar's apparatus for thought and reason and the subsequent projective identificatory processes into the objects in the outside world. It leads at one place to their 'engulfing' the object, which is again then seen as if to 'swell' up so to speak and suffuses and controls the piece of the personality that engulfs it. To that extent, the particle of the personality has become a 'thing' (the goddess) (Bion 1954:345). Kalikinkar's face is in entranced adoration. Doya, Umaprasad, and Khoka are all watching the fireworks, like helpless spectators, in the drama that is to unfold. This manic, frenzied elation is dumped into the depressive core, once the 'music stops.' There is no working through the mourning and giving up of the lost object, to carry on with life in a new way, with the internalisation of the object.

Kalikinkar has lost his mother and his wife. He has not mourned and inter-nalised them. Doya's true self is lost and drowned after the adoration that is to follow. Colonized by the projections that cut out a part of her own apparatus to think, she fits into this Devi image because it serves many purposes.

We now move to the couple's bedroom, where Umaprasad is giving Doya several addressed envelopes to post him letters while he is away at university. Umaprasad is the intellectual with Western values, while Doya is steeped in traditional values and perceptions, like Kalikinkar's. In the banter between them we see her attempt to deal with her anxiety and upset at being left behind. She tries to communicate her anxiety and annoyance, playfully, but he is too excited about his future and cannot understand her anxiety. The edu-cation may be his need, but what about her need? Does she as a woman always have to be the supplier of his need, rather than being the receiver of her need. She never calls out for help or understanding. Has this been silenced within her? This is the brilliance of the movie, so much of the beginning is linked seamlessly into the end, every thread, every word connected. This is so true of our lives. Freud wrote that nothing is ever totally lost, it all remains within the mind, relegated to the unconscious and maybe just lying there, till some event in the present brings it back to life.

Can we then through a beam of darkness, see her concealed anger brewing, that he is choosing to leave and in that act abandoning her. She feels she cannot match him. He is leaving her with his father. In Doya this is the catalyst; her unmetabolized anger ... the impossibility of even knowing it. 'Thoughts without a thinker' (Bion, 1962). There is a moment of some awareness of their shared sexuality, when he mentions that there can be other khokas and she actively nuzzles into him, indicating her wish for her own child. Doya does not smile openly or joyously throughout the film. The only a smile with a slightly open mouth is when she is playing with Khoka. The film tries to show excessive inhibition and repression, not only of sexuality, but of the entire personality. This is also the telescoping of gen-erations (Faimberg, 2005), passed down from mother to daughter – this is how a woman should be. Too much of Doya's will/ego has been split off for her to have any strength to combat it. When does helpless sadness turn into not-so-helpless anger?

The scene now shifts to the temple and a poor devotee with his child is singing a hymn to the goddess. "You gave so much sorrow. I keep calling your name and you turn away, but without you I am forever wretched." This is Kalikinkar's attachment or rather a fusion with his mother. A fusion that has not been metabolized into a space of two people together, yet individuated. Throughout the movie he is heard calling out "ma, ma," in a half-crazed, desperate way – like an infant screaming in panic for the mother. At the same time as this is being sung, Doya is shown doing a puja to the goddess and Kalikinkar totters in again calling out "Ma, Ma, Ma." His walk indicates his physical debility and impotency. He is both the enraged narcissist and the helpless, terrified infant crying out for his mother. Yet, his physical debility does not mean that his sexual desires have been silenced. He looks at Doya, showing a mix of appreciation, gratitude, lust, and maybe even some cunning. His clothing still represents his attempt at being the Lord of the Manor. He yearns for his youth as Doya massages his feet. This is a traditional form of obeisance and acknowledgement of authority of the elderly. He tells Doya, "I hope you don't 'mind' doing these things for me. I know it isn't easy to put up with an old man's whims." The physical touch that relieves his pain, connected with the awareness of the Doya's compassion, stirs up his earliest sense impressions of his mother's loving and comforting touch. His question to Doya shows some awareness that there is something that Doya and he should "mind" what is going on. But both of them are so overtaken by their own unconscious internal happenings, they are not able to make meaning and symbol representation. For both it becomes a symbolic equation – that she is the goddess. When he changes this lust and envy into "pure religious devotion" hence completely sanctioning and serving the original drive. He regains his mother, for Doya becomes this goddess and even the revered mother and joins herself to the father instead of her husband. Kalikinkar prays, "Almighty God cleanse me from within and without. To speak your name is to become pure in body and soul." Somewhere again, he is aware that something needs to be "cleansed," meaning to be made. That his body longs for her youth and the youth of his son and the envy of the young couple. His earliest unresolved oedipal issues, are still strong.

We next see Doya with the parrot. The poor creature with its wings clipped and chained to the rod, can only squawk for his food by calling "Ma." What a parody of Kalikinkar. Doya indulgently strokes it and says, "You must not call on me all the time." Again we see the projective identification and the process of splitting off of awareness. She transfers what she should say to Kalikinkar and says it to the poor hapless and helpless, captive bird, which is also a part of herself. For both protagonists, since the apparatus for thinking has been strangulated, they are only able to make a symbolic equation and act out the fantasy.

Kalikinkar is now shown going to bed, tired, and lying down with the repetition of the word "Ma." At this moment, Doya comes in with his tea and medicine. We can see the unconscious desire in his eyes as he almost seems to leer at her, calls her Little Mother, and asks, "How many have a Mother like that." He tells her of his loss of his wife and his intention of going away on a pilgrimage, but then Doya comes into the house and lights up his life again. He has dealt with his loss, by just sticking the image of his lost mother/wife on to Doya. The goddess has taken the place of his lost wife and mother and from there to making Doya a goddess is a process waiting to happen. A manoeuvre that serves his desire and yet controls it at the same time, preventing oedipal incest.

That night, as Kalikinkar sleeps, he has a dream. On a dark background, two white shapes of eyes appear, and then the third eye which is his own unconscious id impulse. This is exactly what happens when one closes one's eyes and things are reversed; a negative image appears. We know that the last thing he has seen is Doya's eyes and her bindi (dot). The dot then becomes the flames of the prayer lamps, now swirling around in a mesmerising and dizzying manner. We can see these as the beta elements – raw sense impressions, disconnected, things-in-themselves, what Bion calls proto-mental thoughts, not yet converted to rational thoughts which can be a coming together of Sensa, Myth, and Passion. Slowly Doya's face morphs with the three dots and with the circling of the lamps, which is shown in the beginning of the film. He awakens and is puzzled for a brief waking moment and then any attempt to understand the symbolic representation of his dream vanishes. He makes his story, driven by his defence against his oedipal wishes, yet a fulfilment of them; his envious attacks on his son and the young couple, and the restoration of himself as the one in charge and control; the over-determination and his narcissistically driven confabulation. He looks at the photograph of his wife and mother ... again calls out "Ma" and in a hallucinatory state, makes his way to Doya's room. "Why haven't you told us who you are?" He kneels and presses his head to her feet. She is the avatar of Kali. The goddess has come down to stay with him. Having made her the goddess, she will now be in a separate room. No longer in a conjugal relation with his son. Just like an inanimate object, he will control her and put her where he wishes. He has stolen her 'Anima,' her soul. The dream is the fulcrum of the whole movie, linking the past, the present, and what the future is going to be. It is all of the things that Freud wrote that leads to dream formation, the day's residue, the wish fulfilment, the symbol representation, the condensation, and over-determination.

The growth of the infant's mind depends on the loving mother's containing capacity, on her being able in a state of reverie to be receptive to and thus in touch with the incipient meaning to be gleaned from the "raw sensa" of the infantile chaotic, physical, and emotional experience – to acquire the emotional and functional capacities to begin to know the nature of different registers of being and make sense of what he is and what he can bear. Bion proposed that myth, together with sense (sense impressions) and passion (love, hate, and knowledge) in relation to one's primary object, are the three most important defining elements of psychoanalysis. "Myth is the operation of the Alpha function upon those raw sensory and perceptual data that surround the organism, which have to be converted into elements capable of being recorded and stored, before they can become usable for dreaming or myth making" (Levine & Brown, 2013). We can see fragments of the unconscious raw sensory data pressing for their organization and expression in the structure of Kalikinkar's dream. The Oedipal myth relates the themes of love, hate, and incest to the themes of aggression, murder, and guilt, via the knowledge of the Sphinx. Doya, too, is caught in the raw element of this fantasy, unable to bring the force of reason and meaning to resolve her own conflict and rebellion.

Kalikinkar when faced with age and death, chooses delusion as salvation; a narcissistic, retreat of power and fusion with the mother. He therefore can only replace the object with another, as if it were the same with no re-cognition of the characteristics of the original object and his own relationship to it in reality. He is 'His Majesty the Baby,' who expects to be worshipped by the mother and projects the desire to be worshipped on to the idol and worships it as a replacement of the lost object. It is not internalized to reside forever within his heart with its own individual persona. Andre Green (1986) in his book *On Private Madness*, points out that the coexistence between the psychotic and neurotic parts of the personality may be the result of a situation of sterile stalemate between the Reality Principle and the sexual libido on the one hand and the Pleasure Principle and aggressive libido on the other. For Kalikinkaar, his primitive drives force themselves forward once again into the empty space left by the death of his wife and the loss of his youth and physical vigour. His fantasy represents a compulsive activity to fill this void.

He now sets her up in a separate sanctum, as a goddess to be worshipped. A doubting priest performs the sanctification. We see a confused, but totally submissive Doya letting it all happen. The myth becomes the fulcrum for the enactment of the turbulent emotional and mental conflicts in society as well as in the family. How much the external affects the internal and vice versa. The whole process of acting out instead of 'thinking' is set in process. Soon a villager brings his dying child and places it in her lap. Miraculously, the child, who had not opened his eyes for days, opens his eyes. He is declared as cured. As news spreads, the sick and the poor come seeking cures. She is now a prisoner in her own home. We see this externally as internally in her mind. She appeals to her sister-in-law to write to her husband of what is happening. Umaprasad returns home and tries to reason with his father, but to no avail. Kalikinkar sticks with his 'belief.' Kalikinkar now has the look of a mad man. Umaprasad tells him, "You have gone mad." Kalikinkar says, "So I am out of my mind?" There seems to some weak attempt by the ego to re-establish the Reality Principle, but the hallucination/delusion is too strong and responds, "No, I am not mad. Shall I recite the Gita (Prayer Book) for you? No one's worthier of respect than one's own father. Pay honour to your Father if you would honour the Gods; The paternal spirit is more radiant than the Sun," etc. As he speaks his voice gains strength. Umaprasad asks, "How did you know that she is an incarnation?" and Kalikinkar replies that he had a vision. Umaprasad responds, "And all this is based on just one dream?" Of course we know that his dream is a culmination of days, months, and years of gestation in the realm of the unconscious. Uma is totally disbelieving, but he cannot get his father to give up his delusion. He goes to Doya's room. He finds her confused and undecided about whether she really is the incarnation or not. He speaks to her lovingly and understandingly, saying, she is too young to protest, to say anything. He will not let her go on with this. He has arranged for a boat at the river's edge and they can escape. At night, he protectively leads her to the river edge, holding her and supporting her. Then suddenly she stops. They have come upon the bamboo frame backdrop on which the goddess had been carried to the river for immersion. Towards the end of the film we come back to it. A message – the idol is just an idol, an illusion ... after it is gone, what are you left with. No real internalization, just a void and an empty space. She is now overcome with doubts. On looking at it, Doya falters and Uma is stunned to find that she thinks that maybe the Goddess has entered into her after all. "What if I am an incarnation, the child was cured, he opened his eyes?" Umaprasad says, "What does that prove? One hears of many such 'cures.' Once you are away from here, your doubts will disappear." But she pleads, "Don't make me leave this way. I am afraid, take me back...." and makes him take her back. Meanwhile, Khoka falls very ill and somehow, nobody calls the doctor. This Bion's Group functioning under the Basic Assumption (mental state) of Dependency. He remains the omnipotent leader, by controlling all the financial and physical assets of the family members, keeping them needing him. They do not wish to give up this comfort and work for their own individuation. Kalikinkar places the unconscious Khoka in Doya's lap, where Khoka breathes his last.

Umaprasad tries to take her away, but Doya has lost all reason in this confused psychotic state. She is shown running into the field and disappearing into the mist; maybe into the same river into which we see the face of the revered idol slowly submerging and disappearing at the beginning of the film. Here is the complete dissolution of Doya's own identity and life. It reminds me of Hans Christian Andersen's fairy tale *The Shadow and the Master*. The True Self fades away as it gets further and further away from Truth and Reality and the Shadow; the False Self becomes the Master grown enormous with the feeding of Lies which then affect True Self and leave it emaciated and overwhelmed. Rosenfeld (1950) writes about the "Psychopathology of Confusional States," where good and bad objects cannot be kept apart and are confused. "These infantile states of confusion are states of disintegration and are related to confusional schizoid states of the adult. The confusional state is associated with extreme anxiety because when the libidinal and aggressive impulses become confused, the destructive impulses seem to threaten and destroy the libidinal impulse. Consequently, the whole self is in danger of being destroyed. If normal differentiation cannot be achieved, splitting mechanisms become reinforced, the libidinal and aggressive impulses become confused, the destructive impulses seem to threaten to destroy the libidinal impulse" (133).

What makes Doya stay in this horrible incarceration of her spirit and very existence? What makes her submit? What has created this scotoma in her mind; the truth she does not wish to see? Is it some sado/masochistic impulse, through which she will not forgive Umaprasad for leaving her? So while Doya is shown as the meek, loving, and compassionate part, what about her part in the destruction of Umaprasad's life and his love? Sometimes one notices something by its absence, like a Black Hole, the anger and hatred that cannot be seen or known. Is she now so caught up in a folie a deux and shared this hallucination with Kalikinkar because it makes her become the powerful one where people bow at her feet instead of her having to bow to them? With his powerful projections into her, is she a willing receptor? Is it also the fulfilment of her joint oedipal wish along with Kalikinkar, now possible because no actual sexuality can come in and so it can proceed without guilt? Does that ominous bamboo frame lying discarded in the mud flats represent her inability now to live without her goddess avatar? When her delusion is no longer possible to maintain, Doya seeks refuge in insanity and maybe even suicide (the movie leaves it to us to conjecture the end). It reminds us of Freud's words at the end of the Schreber paper. He created another world, not more grand it is true, but at least one that he could live in. The beta elements of uncontainable sense impressions are channeled into some pathology, whereby they can be contained without overt madness or breakdown. But when it no longer works, there is a danger of liquidation and disintegration of the personality.

To conclude, as Green says, does not mean to close the work, but to open the discussion and to leave the floor to others.

References

Bion, W.R. (1954). Notes on a Theory of Schizophrenia. *Int. J. Psychoanal.*, 35:113–118.
Alvarez, A. (1998). Failures to Link: Attacks or Defects: Some Questions concerning Thinkability of Oedipal and Pre-Oedipal Thoughts. *J. Child Psychother.*, 24(2):213–231.
Bion, W.R. (1956). Development of Schizophrenic Thought. *Int. J. Psychoanal.*, 37:344–348.
Bion, W.R. (1957). Differentiation of the Psychotic from the Non-Psychotic Personalities. *Int. J. Psychoanal.*, 38:266–275.
Bion, W.R. (1959). Attacks on Linking. *Int. J. Psychoanal.*, 40:308–315.
Bion, W.R. (1962). A Psycho-Analytic Study of Thinking. *Int. J. Psychoanal.*, 43:306–310.
Bion, W.R. (1970). *Attention and Interpretation: A Scientific Approach to Insight in Psychoanalysis and Groups.* London: Routledge.
Faimberg, H. (2005). *The Telescoping of Generations.* London: Routledge.
Green, A. (1986). *A Private Madness.* Madison, CT: International University Press, Inc..
Korbivcher, C.F. (2013). Bion and Tustin: The Autistic Phenomenon. *Int. J. Psychoanal.*, 94(4):645–665.
Levine, H. & Brown, L.J. (2013). *Growth and Turbulence in the Container/Contained: Bion's Continuing Legacy.* London: Routledge.
Rosenfeld, H. (1950). Notes on the Psychopathology of Confusional States in Chronic Schizophrenia. *Int. J. Psychoanal.*, 31:132–137.

Part V

Introduction for intimacy and violence

Gertraud Schlesinger-Kipp

This section brings together two at the first sight totally different topics, the psychotherapeutic approach to female refugees in Germany and the fight of for more intimacy and pleasure for women in psychiatric hospitals in India. But both texts are about the deprivation of human rights for women. In the first article Gertraud Schlesinger-Kipp describes how women are forced to leave their home country not only for the same reason as men, war, hunger, political oppression, but also for specific female reasons like forced marriage, rape, FGM (female genital mutilation), total deprivation of right for education, working, and liberty.

Female refugees on their flight are even more in danger then men. Female inhabitants in psychiatric hospitals in India are even more deprived of any possibility of pleasure, sexuality, and relationship with a partner as the patriarchal system in India does not see them as potential partners for men. Homosexual relationships were forbidden and persecuted until shortly after this Congress. Ambulatory and half-closed living facilities for psychotic patients do not exist. Ratnaboli Ray describes how these women blossom after being part of a project.

This chapter wants to encourage psychotherapists and social workers to be on the side of the underprivileged women all over the world.

8 Sorrow, pain, loss, trauma … Psychosocial and psychotherapeutic approaches with female refugees

Gertraud Schlesinger-Kipp

A. Introduction

After the international conference of the IPA in Boston 2015, during which a lot was said on the challenges to psychoanalysis in this changing world, we Germans came back to another rapidly changing reality. Escaping the terror of the IS, not drowning in the Mediterranean like so many others, fleeing the tent cities in Lebanon, Jordan, and Turkey by the millions, hiking around the Hungarian barbed wire fences in the mud, they ended up with us (1.1 million in 2015, Germany). The causes for escaping and taking refuge in this world exist not only since this summer, but the misery had not been this clear and close for a long time.

Threats of fear, which today show in the fear of Islam in Europe, are nothing new. But Berlinghoff (Institute of migration research and intercultural studies, University of Osnabrück, Germany) emphasizes: "Migration has always taken place in human history. Behind the idea that cultures, ethnic groups, peoples or nations are not compatible with each other, there is the image of fixed units, which they are not de facto. "In Europe, too, everything was constantly in flux. When societies remain static, they perish. Societies live through exchange" (Thorsten Harmsen, Berliner Zeitung 23.9.17).

However, the refugee movement is on the increase: more than 65 million people worldwide were refugees in 2016, most flee within the country, and only a small percentage flee to Europe or even reach Europe. Eighty-four percent of refugees live in poor countries.

B. Frame of volunteer work

Alexander and Margarete Mitscherlich were psychoanalysts who meddled in the present after World War II. So perhaps it is no coincidence that at the psychoanalytical institute in Kassel, which is called the Alexander Mitscherlich Institute, in the fall of 2015 to today 20–25 psychoanalysts, as well as psychiatrists and psychotherapists and child and adolescent analysts have come together to share our feelings and fears and thoughts, not to be alone with the news and pictures on TV of the thousands of refugees coming every day to Germany.

The refugees who are there should be handled with human dignity, and that is for us to do, to offer them our knowledge and commitment. In the countries where the refugees come from, there are dehumanizing states and experiences, not only in the war but also on the escape route and now at our border fences and now in Germany as well. We believe that psychoanalysis and we as people can approach the question and try to understand how these dehumanizing processes affect the individual, now and in the long term. This means also not to dehumanize ourselves. We know from trauma research that the manner with which the refugees are welcomed or not is essential for their further psychic and social development. The big difference to the mass migration in many other countries of the world is here in Europe that there are different cultures, religions, and languages, so the integration process is crucial for the larger society.

It is not allowed to offer them psychotherapy or other treatment except emergency treatment. But the local district authority has given us the permission, which was not the case in other cities. Our group first met with the attending physician and psychiatrist to discuss why we do this volunteer work, about our helplessness and desperation in the face of the often arbitrary bureaucracy, in addition to offering encouragement to each other to continue our work to help people in need. We were fortunate that the authority was a psychiatrist who had confidence in us.

One colleague articulated her motivation: "One can live in Kassel without having seen even one refugee more than from afar. But I cannot, I cannot and do not want to cut myself off from what's happening in society."

We consider what has developed to be more than psychosocial help, since it is a different approach from psychotherapy in the traditional sense. Most often we see refugees with post-traumatic stress disorder, which is the after-effect of the often traumatic experiences in the home countries and on the run, as well as sometimes here in Germany. Almost as often we were also presented with residents with depression, anxiety, and panic disorders, which sometimes existed previously in their home country (just as often symptoms were related to marital and family problems). From trauma research, we know that the type of experience that refugees have upon their arrival is of great importance for their further development. This concerns admission procedures, interviews, living conditions, medical treatment, and waiting times; for the most part missing psychosocial and psychotherapeutic care, returns, threats, etc.

Meanwhile, we are increasingly working with the psychological consequences of the uncertainty caused by the intensified transportation practice of the Germany federal government. Even mentally ill asylum seekers who are severely traumatized can now be deported. So far, they could at least receive a subsidiary protection. However now only a serious physical illness which prevents the pure transportability is a transportation obstacle. Afghans who grew up in Iran and were never in Afghanistan, who have nothing and nobody there, can also be transported back. Women who first entered Europe in Italy and were caught there by human trafficking and forced into prostitution and managed to flee to Germany, may be transported to Italy again because the European law states refugees have to remain in the country where they first entered. Due to fear, aggression, psychosomatic illnesses, suicide attempts and suicides, and enormous tensions in the camps, people retreat into one's own four walls in the apartments and depression, obsessions, and delusions can increase enormously.

Escape and gender

According to the council of German psychotherapists, about 40% of the refugees are mentally ill or traumatized.

One-third of all refugees, who in January 2016 for the first time applied for asylum in Germany, are women and girls. They leave their homeland necessarily for the same reasons as men: war, bombed cities, villages under ISIS rule, no water, no electricity, no food, no future, shattered lives, and political oppression. There are also gender-specific reasons for escape: domestic violence, forced marriages, female genital mutilation, and honor killings. For women, the escape is on foot, in unfit boats, in trains, and usually more dangerous than for men. They are even more exposed to physical, sexual, and psychic violence than are men. Even in the refugee camps, many run the risk of suffering sexual violence by partners, residents, or even personnel. While the men try to be mobile, women almost never leave their accommodations out of fear and because in their countries of origin it was not common to walk alone in the street.

Since 1951 (the Geneva Convention), gender-related persecution applies as a reason for asylum, but this was only recognized since 2005 by the Immigration Act in Germany. In reality, last year out of more than 33,000 applicants for asylum in Germany, only 624 were recognized because of 'gender-related persecution' in their home country. These were women and also homosexual men. Often proof is required that the women cannot bring.

In all wars from ancient times on, rape of women and other forms of sexual violence was and is used by the war combatants to destroy procreation, to serve the soldiers, to fuse one's genes into the enemy, to humiliate the enemy, and to attack the most fragile part of the enemy, women and girls. In many countries, women are considered as less valuable and less worthy as individuals. Fatal outcomes of this are more homicides and suicides, more unintended pregnancies, miscarriages and stillbirth, preterm delivery and low-birth-weight babies. Often in young mothers, there is depression, post-traumatic stress and other disorders, sleep and eating disorders, psychosomatic problems such as headaches, back pain, and fibromyalgia; psychic and actual retreat and poor overall health also occurs (Varvin, 2016).

A. **Attempt of a conceptualisation of frequently single therapeutic discussions with refugee women in the initial reception (see Straker, 1990)**

Conceptualisation of often only one-time conversations with refugees

1. Opening of the conversation:

    –   Building up trust
    –   Introduction by confidant (interpreter)
    –   Secrecy, volunteer work, no political authority

2. Trauma

    –   'What was the worst?' Individual traumatic story
    –   Respect the unspeakable
    –   Refugee should not be overwhelmed by painful emotions
    –   Sympathy, expressing compassion

3. Relieve feelings of shame and guilt

    –   Shame by identity and dignity loss
    –   Shame as a victim of violence
    –   De-pathologizing
    –   Survival guilt

4. End of the conversation

    –   Do not leave in helpless situation
    –   Address resources and coping
    –   Discuss practical help

In the following text, I will bring examples from treatment sessions with refugees in camps or in the psychosocial center to illustrate this conceptualisation.

1. **Opening the conversation:**

    Building up trust
    The situation, from which the refugees come, including the escape itself, is reason enough for suspicion and distrust. The consultant is not exempt from this distrust. In addition, the refugees are often unfamiliar with psychotherapy and counseling. For this reason it is important that we are introduced to the refugee by a trustworthy person. Often this is the interpreters who spent a lot of time in the facility noticing nearly everything. In addition, we carry out our idea of voluntary independent interviewing, including maintaining the confidentiality, once this is desired by them. It is definitely important to emphasize that we are not appointed by the authorities, but work freely and voluntarily and we only intervene if it is requested by the refugee. (Otherwise – very often later, when refugees stay longer here, you hear only sometimes made-up sentences, which will allow them to stay in Germany.)

    In contrast to the otherwise necessary attitude of abstinence of psychotherapists, the therapist should express their political and personal solidarity, their opinion against violence and war, as one of the objectives to transform the private suffering of a violence victim into public suffering. The victim must deprivatise his suffering. The governmental and/or terrorist violence has often meant that these men, women, and children fell ill individually. Privatisation is exactly the goal of the oppressors. It's not about politicising away the individual suffering but about incorporating an appropriate consideration of both personal and social issues in the therapy or treatment.

2. Trauma

After discussing the catastrophe in general, depending upon our evaluation, we can ask for the individual traumatic story, and always include the question of whether they want to talk about it. One can ask, for example, if they want to tell, what the worst part of it was. At the same time it is crucial to make sure that the refugee is not overwhelmed by his emotions. The interpreter's presence is often useful. It already happened to me that an interpreter said: "This question I do not translate because she would collapse." This may provide a conjoint defense, as the trauma is extremely taboo in the camps. It is very helpful in this situation of only one conversation, to include the interpreter as they frequently come from a similar culture and possibly similar experiences. Often enough, the taboo nature of the trauma in the institutions is a common defense. Workers and interpreters say "they all are traumatized" but no one talks about it. We needed also to give some knowledge about trauma, for example that it is a relief even in the situation of the camp to express something in a protected space.

Respecting the unspeakable: Even in the protected area far from the site of traumatic experiences, it may happen that victim and therapist both lose their capacity to verbalise the experiences because the therapists can become carriers of emotions. It is therefore important that the therapists themselves are not exposed to this terror and are not at the point of danger, being aware that the physical pains are not really to share. We experience just a small grade of the awe. But it is important to respect the limits of the fear of talking about.

As therapists, we provide the refugees a shelter through our presence and support. He should not be overwhelmed by painful emotions. It is important that we as therapists do not remain remote, but express our sympathy without overwhelming ourselves. Life in the camp infects everybody who works there, mostly of course those who are present all the time: the manager, the helpers, the paramedics, and the interpreters. And so it does to us who are there only briefly but regularly. The manager put it aptly: "If anything is wrong with us – the staff and paramedics – or if I'm not in a good mood, then something happens." That is certainly true, as well as in psychiatric wards, on the other hand it mirrors the taking over of guilty feelings many refugees suffer.

Dari

Dari (see also Sé Holovko & Schlesinger-Kipp, 2019) is 33 years old. I encountered a soft, pretty, young woman with only a light cloth over her head. The interview was conducted with the help of the interpreter. We asked her what had happened in the other camp. We only know that she was brought here with her children, and was separated from her husband. She tells us rather emotionless that she lived in one room with the two younger children, a girl of 11 years and a 5-year-old boy, while her husband lived next door with the 14-year-old son. Her husband used to drink and then beat the son. She had heard sounds from their room, and then the police arrived. I asked her whether that happened before and she affirms. Her husband would beat their son heavily, even at home. He would use cables and scissors – the son had many scars.

She tells us, without our asking, that it was not a good relationship at all. Her husband would not regard her as his wife; he would be more like a father. I ask her what she meant. She says she had been married at the age of 10 years. I look at her incredulously – married at the age of 10? She says yes, she could show me. I say, I believe her, I knew that this happened, but I have never met anyone to whom this happened. She corrects herself, she had been engaged at 10 and married at 13, clearly still a child. She played outside when her parents came to her and said, "Now you marry this man." He is 10 years older than her. He never talked to her or respected her in any way; only told her to do this and do that. It was bad. She then says that she had lied to him during their flight, had said she wanted to stay with him. But that was not true.

I ask her if she wants to separate. She says she did not want to live with him until the son is 18 or until the kids are grown up, but could she possibly separate without a divorce? I nod. She was afraid because a brother of her husband at home was a bit crazy and could do harm to her family. I ask her if her husband had been drinking at home, too. She says he had taken drugs there, here he would drink instead. He had always gone away with his friends, had never cared for her and the children. Has he also beaten her and the other children? Yes, the daughter sometimes – she does not talk about herself. He would be interested only in the boys, did not care about her and the girl. I wonder why he beats his son so badly if he would be so important to him?

Indeed she decided to leave her country in order to separate from her husband. For the first time, she shows emotions and cries a little. I dig in my pocket for a handkerchief. There has not been a single happy day in her life with him. Again I ask her if she really wants to live again with that man whom she had to marry as a child, who beats his son, who mistreats her – once her son would have grown up?! The interpreter says she has been at the Youth Office with the family, that's all I know. Dari does not know where her eldest son is, she says. They have taken him elsewhere. She would like to know where he is and how he is doing. She should not know that, because the children would be calling the father and perhaps tell him. I promised that I would ask the camp leader.

Now she wants to say, she has decided that she would no longer live with her husband. She says it three times. In her culture, a word is only valid if you repeat it three times. She looks determined, but something feels wrong.

After the interview the interpreter is quite taken. She did not know there is something like forced marriage in childhood.

I talk to the social worker. She reports that she has been at the Youth Office with the family. "Nobody would ever understand our statutes of child protection!" she says. Child Protection Services have taken the 14-year-old in custody. The mother is not allowed to have contact with the husband; otherwise, the other children would also be taken away. I am a bit angry that I did not know all this before the interview. Well, perhaps this is fortunate because she would not have opened up like she did and the conversation might have focussed on the prohibition of contact. At least she had to think for herself about what she wanted. But I really wonder what is true.

3. **Discharge of shame and guilt**

Many victims of war, trauma, torture, and escape blame themselves subjectively for the consequences of trauma. A woman from Syria kept saying: "I'm not strong enough." A hasty appeasement that she could have done nothing does not help, but rather, asking what she thinks she could have done and failed in her opinion. Only then can she distinguish between subjective interpretation of her guilt and possibly actually existing alternatives. Of course the political context is of great importance and too often we know little or what we know is one-sided. It is important not to behave didactically, since the refugee knows the situation so much better, and often so does the interpreter.

The shame about the experience of complete loss of identity, the loss of one's own values and the ego-ideal, to have submitted without contours, cannot be discussed in a normal conversational situation. Each person has his/her own "levels of shame": first something turns up that might be called the "loss of face," to have fallen out of the natural social context. After that, shame is about not having foreseen the situation. Finally, the shame appears of what was mentioned here, the panic shame to be submerged by a loss of identity and submission. The question would be how it is possible to convert our basic sense of shame in useful signals to defend being penetrated by the disastrous inhumanity of our time?

De-pathologization: The symptoms and complaints are often a normal reaction to the abnormal traumatic experience. Many believe that they have lost their mental health because of their symptoms, were becoming insane, and no one could help them any more. Knowing that one is still normal and that the symptoms will disappear with time is a great relief.

Hana

Hana is 20 years old and far along in her pregnancy. She has mainly grown up in Africa in a refugee camp. She had then fled from there to Libya and fell into the hands of Chad rebels. She had been detained in a camp. The men there were mistreated heavily, the women raped. She, too, had been raped repeatedly and injured, too. She was able then to buy out with money at a tout (an accomplice?) and take flight across the Mediterranean.

Hana at first hesitates to talk about these incidents. She says she was always ashamed when she is asked about her pregnancy, where the father is. She does not know who the father is. She seems very quiet, depressed, absent, very composed, and controlled. She notes in hints that she does not know how she could accept the child. She did not have anybody at her side. She would sleep poorly though physically she had no problems with pregnancy.

I make a long pause and think about what I can say to this friendly, humiliated woman. I tell her then that it would not be for her to feel ashamed, but that the shame belongs to the perpetrators. I say this very firmly and twice: "You've gone through terrible experiences, but now you will have a child soon and that also offers a future." She relaxes somewhat and can describe her feelings of shame in a restrained way. And she says: "I will say now that the father is still in Africa."

The interpreter said that he often saw her sitting somewhere seeming totally absent. This is probably the reason why she was introduced to me only then, despite living in the camp for months – she does not attract attention.

Meanwhile, Hana has given birth to her baby. The birth was a Caesarean section with complications. When she came back to the camp after 14 days, all were very happy and excited and made a party for her. She accepts and takes care of her baby and breastfeeds very well. But as soon as she is alone, she has this empty, lost look in her eyes again. She was transferred to another camp, quite far away and the camp leader and interpreter visited her for the baptism of the child.

4. **In the end** of the conversation, it is important that the refugee is not left in a helpless, overpowered situation, but is able to talk about their current concerns and problems, and is provided with practical assistance, and encouraged to establish contact with relatives. One can also offer questions about whether this conversation has helped and whether others (family members, for example) would also benefit from it, etc. Also important is to emphasise the importance of one's own opinion and to put their suffering in a larger context, along with encouragements about what they can do for themselves and their own ideas about their circumstances.

Activation of resources: It is important to show to the victim that in spite of persecution and war she has succeeded to survive mentally and to escape. That despite the experience of exposure to violence she was capable to reject the role of being the sufferer, being defeated and overpowered, and instead start acting for themselves.

5. **Practical help and powerlessnes**

For many refugees, the encounter with someone who exposes himself to their strangeness is already a bit healing. At least we thought we believed in this in the beginning when we went to the initial reception centers and then founded the association's Psychosocial Center for Refugees. But more and more it turns out for us that we can hardly help, that the uncanny for us grows in our own society. The change in the climate against the refugees, the more aggressive asylum and transportation policy of the federal government is for us uncanny.

Ali

A very young man, a survivor of torture and sexual violence, suffers from post-traumatic stress disorder with symptoms such as flashbacks, anxiety, and shame, and, presumably, self-harm. He wakes up and has head and arm injuries without knowing what happened. He is very afraid of men.

By working in the kitchen in the accommodations he is reasonably stable. At the age of 13 he was sold by his employer to men who tortured him and then he had to work as an imprisoned dance girl. These are boys, after their sexual maturity (before sex with children is prohibited here, children at 13 whether boy or girl are considered man and woman), disguised as girls to have to dance for men and are then raped. He often tried to take his own life during the two years, but was always rescued and received medical treatment. He managed to plan his escape when he heard men talking about Europe. He cannot tell his family; such boys are like lepers forever, and the neighbors would kill him. I try to arrange a stay in a shelter for women who suffered from human trafficking, but of course they are limited to accepting only women.

Due to his extreme past history, he belongs to the most vulnerable group of refugees who require special treatment according to EU guidelines which typically are not respected by the authorities. Shortly after the first encounter with me, the young man was to be transferred despite my statement that he is not moveable. He committed a very serious suicidal attempt and was transferred into the psychiatric clinic (often the last hope of shelter for the very vulnerable). Fortunately, the psychiatric hospital was able to accept him and his story seriously, was sensitive to his fear of men and allowed him to stay for a few weeks, typically not the norm. (The fact that he even talks about this story suggests he needed a lot of work on his shame. In the first interview for asylum in front of men of the authority he could not say anything about his torture.) After the psychiatric hospital, the young man (despite our efforts) was transferred to a remote rural area during the night.

Present and future

The Balkan route was closed and the refugees were stopped and lived under inhuman conditions in Greece and along the border of Greece and other European countries (like Hungarian and Serbia which closed their borders). The political atmosphere has changed a lot, and nationalism, racism, and xenophobia have increased.

In June 2017, the NGO boats and official Frontex boats rescued in three days more than 8,900 people. In this half year, more than 73,000 arrived in Italy, which feels left alone by all other EU countries and announces that they will not let the boats into Italian harbors anymore. Thousands drowned this year (more than 5,000 in 2016). The ones who survive live in inhumane conditions in Italy. Now (in 2019), all the NGO boats are no longer there to rescue drowning people. The harbors in Italy are closed for them; the skippers themselves were sometimes put in jail. Frontex (the official organization by the European Union) brings the little boats back to the Libyan border (and from there back to the Libyan camps and jails with inhuman conditions, torture, rape, and hunger). We do not know how many refugees are drowning and we do not know what their names are. And when we hear something, there is no cry anymore in the public; there is the routine of indifference.

Conclusion

Presentness, which includes and allows for the past and the future, could benefit from the experiences that elders in Germany have had living as children in a dictatorial system and in a world war. Their losses, traumas, new beginnings, upheavals, silent and speechless parents, and teachers can be of great value to those who have fled today. Likewise, through our past in our families, we may also be particularly afraid of the loss of identity, of being at home, and of being lost in the world. The refugees who have lost everything make us inwardly touched by this fear. Working with them, professionally or voluntarily, or both, requires the willingness to face this shock. Joshua Durban, an Israeli psychoanalyst who is working with Syrian and Lebanese refugees in Israel, puts it this way:

> Our sense of home, having a home or being at home, seems as natural to us as the air we breathe. It is as natural to us as our physical and mental existence. To live somewhere, not to be alone, to be seen and understood, is part of our humanity. And yet this is an important achievement of our development, which we should not take for granted." And later "to these unimaginable fears are the threat of being a limited psycho-biological entity; having neither an interior nor an appearance, to run out, to become empty, to melt, to freeze, to burn, to fall, to dissolve, no sense of space and time.
>
> (Durban, 2017)

Against these unimaginable fears that Durban calls 'nowhereness,' there are various defenses: finding an object that is a human being who can become a real, development-promoting object that gives the refugee a protective screen, a kind of home. Or, against this unimaginable anxiety, you can face a rigid, impenetrable layer of protection that uses weapons, ideologies to externalize your fears, to burn, dissolve, freeze, and banish the other...

Could it be a whole society is having these two possibilities? That's why the refugees, who are seen as living examples of our own unimaginable fears, must be so repulsive, encapsulated, and sent back, exiled.

An attempt to be a home for them temporarily is our project despite our powerlessness. 'Death guilt' (Peskin, 2015) thrives on the compulsive re-petition of self-doubt that doubles the past into the future. 'Life guilt' has the imperative to make the future better, to know what to do and what not to do. The ethos of 'death guilt,' to do no harm only leads to the disengagement and reproach-free distancing of injustices, to the melancholy debt discourse and retreat from the present. 'Life guilt,' on the other hand, leads to rela-tional involvement, responsibility for actions in the present. Not more nor less is our project.

References

Durban, J. (2017). Home, homelessness and nowhere-ness in early infancy. *Journal of Child Psychotherapy, 43*(2): 175-191.

Harmsen, T., Berliner Zeitung 23.9.17.

Peskin, H. (2017). Uses of guilt in the treatment of dehumanization. *The International Journal of Psychoanalysis, 98*(2): 473–489.

Schlesinger-Kipp, G.: About presence DPV Proceedings Spring 2015, (authors edition).

Sé Holovko, C., Schlesinger-Kipp, G. (2019). Speaking of sexual abuse with female re-fugees, in Harris, A. Montagna, P. *Psychoanalysis, law and society*, in print.

Straker, G. (1990). Permanent mental stress as traumatic syndrome - a unique therapeutic conversation. *Psyche 44*(2): 144–163.

Varvin, Sverre. (2016). Asylsuchende und Geflüchtete: ihre Situation und ihre Behandlunsgbedürfnisse, *Psyche, Z Psychoanal*, Heft 9:825. ff.

9 Pleasure, politics, and 'pagalpan'

Ratnaboli Ray

I'm sharing this story because it's happening within a mental institution. All of us must have fallen in love with our doctor, at some point in our lives, and this story is happening within an institution where love is completely forbidden, it's illicit, and if your love story becomes public, i.e., if you're exposed, then what is going to happen? The psychiatrist is going to increase your medication, the nursing staff would take away the lovely clothes that you wear and would like to wear, the Group D staff may feed you less and even withdraw your toiletries, and what can then happen? Let's think for a moment of the environment of a public mental hospital; there is so much filth, dirt, squalor, that you are allowed to dwell in that filth, and this is perhaps a deliberate ploy by the mental health institution because filth and dirt and squalor can make you further unseen, by extension, your body is hidden, and therefore, the binary that we look in institution regarding sexuality and sexual expression is sex object versus sex absent, and that is really problematic, and a huge concern.

I don't think we have a concern particularly with medication, but the way medical sciences is played out within an institution is a problem. Maybe medication needs to be given, but what is problematic is the normalising of the fact that you will not have sexual desires, the 'okay-ness' of it bothers us a lot, and how do we deal with this 'okay-ness,' to make it not okay, is our question.

Many of the women in the ward actually work in the canteen we have opened up in the mental health institution, and every time they come to the workplace, they need to be groomed, they need to be dressed, they put on their kajal, and lipstick, and they have to encounter comments like, 'Oh! So you are going to look at men!' Jarring words as if pursuing a man is a sin, and pursuing a woman is not even in their imagination.

They have also spent years in isolation, which amplifies their feelings of pain and suffering, and if they then crave for touch, it is considered inappropriate and they feel it is a punishment because then they start to feel more vulnerable. And why do we pathologise touch? Why is it restricted, forbidden, or prohibited for women or men within mental health institutions, because skin is a large organ of our body, and we need to be touched, and skin hunger will obviously give rise to other issues around mental health or may exaggerate mental health conditions.

They are asked about what they are going to do with their sexual lives and sexual expression and what they are not going to do within the institution, and one of the women said, "Nobody told me what to do and what not to do in my marriage, and I was married for 10 years before I came to the institution, so why is it that now I am being told what to do, and what not to do, and I feel like a child, and is this fair?"

Is it that we really feel that 120 women in the female ward of a government mental hospital will start masturbating at the same time? And it brings me to a very important point about pleasure. What is pleasure? When I talk about pleasure, I mean all the things I talked about from love, clothes, lipstick, food; everything is pleasure. It is not about just appeasement of your body, and therefore access to pleasure, it is perhaps the most important access issue that we talk about. It's not just about infrastructure, or treatment, or care. The recovery model also has ramifications in the way we practitioners address issues of sexuality because it means that people have a choice and a right to take risks and they have a right to fail, and we shouldn't have any judgments whether the outcomes are positive or negative, whether they will regret it later or not, and therefore access to pleasure is the most important accessible issue within psychosocial disability; let's focus on pleasure, which is not just one kind of pleasure, but many different kinds of pleasure.

The dilemma that I have is the proverbial dilemma with public and private. How much of these narratives can I make public because these are highly private narratives and we have all the details. Even for a moment if I borrow the enduring slogan of 'personal is political,' it is important whose story we are bringing out in the public, and who is making that public, and whether I have the right as a practitioner to make those stories public, for transformation because if I make my story public, I have the power and I come from a position of privilege, where I can deal with the onslaught. But I am unsure that vulnerable as they are, institution stories come out in the public, whether they will be able to deal with the onslaught or backlash and whether it is right for us.

Conclusion

Jhuma Basak, Paula L. Ellman, and
Gertraud Schlesinger-Kipp

Conclusion by Jhuma Basak.

By the time one reached the concluding part of working process of the present book, *Psychoanalytic and Socio-Cultural Perspectives on Women in India: Violence, Safety, and Survival* based on the first COWAP meet in Kolkata, 2018, the city had successfully hosted the second COWAP meet in 2019. The initial dialogue revolving around women, psychoanalysis, social sciences, society, culture, and politics prompted the discourse on "women in romance, sex, and marriage" in its second convocation in Kolkata. This was met with equal fierceness in participation from different parts of India, the world, and from various professionals coming from disciplines including mental health, social sciences, activists, research scholars, and the student community. The evolving new India is gradually becoming a growing ground for its women as the new community leaders of the country. A striking precedent may be found in the protests led by women across India as the "Shaheen Bagh Protests" from mid-December 2019 voicing against the citizenship amendment act passed by the government that alleged discrimination against Muslims and other minority communities of the country. It resonated innumerable peace meetings led by women across the country for months, protesting for the inclusion of all castes and tribes as legitimate citizens of India. Most unfortunately, the sudden attack of the COVID-19 pandemic in India from March 2020 shook all grounds for mankind across the world. When a global crisis like COVID-19 storms over civilization with such swift measures against all preparation, then all other preceding human concerns and struggles probably take secondary consideration. And that's exactly how the Shaheen Bagh Movement was left half-way for the emerging community leaders of this country. Human race was left with only one singular engagement – to survive the threat to human life by the coronavirus. In the near future, whenever it may be that the COVID-19 situation stabilises, one hopes that the rising women of India will once again regain their spirit to march for their rights, equality, and justice and fight with all their zeal to attain their present position of authority and direction.

Concluding remarks by Paula L. Ellman

This book, *Psychoanalytic and Socio-Cultural Perspectives on Women in India: Violence, Safety, and Survival* is a compilation of rich, evocative chapters connecting with the culture, history, myths, and literature along with a psychoanalytic perspective on India with its primary focus on the safety of women. Contributors include psychoanalysts, psychologists, social scientists, research scholars, and activists coming together to offer an experience of immersion in this crucial topic in our world today. This book's contributions of chapters are from the presenters at the first IPA COWAP Conference in Kolkata, India, creatively and effectively organised by Dr. Jhuma Basak with her planning committee. She and her committee had a vision to address the problem of the '*Safety of Women in Dogmatic Times* in early spring 2018 and "sold out" every space for attendees two months in advance of the scheduled conference date. With the tremendous interest that this conference evoked in the Indian community, Dr. Basak organized a second IPA COWAP Conference in November 2019 on *Women in Romance, Sex and Marriage,* which garnered just as much interest with its rich, lively presentations and full attendance. The conferences and this edited collection have a significance in India that allow for the voice of women that has not been heard, especially in times of dogma and patriarchy.

Since the submission of this edited book to the publisher, our global world has markedly changed with the appearance of COVID-19. While the pandemic and its social effects therefore were not under consideration by the authors in this book, now is an opportunity to take note of our changed world before the actual publication of this book. The virus entered our worlds and infiltrated existing social fractures. The nature of the virus's effects highlights already-existing social problems. COVID-19 shines a light on the social disparities within the social weavings that are already in place. While we all have been profoundly affected by the pandemic in our concerns about safety and impact on our lifestyles, those most affected by it, those that are dying disproportionately, are those that are marginalised: the poor, the disadvantaged, the vulnerable not only medically but also socially. In actuality, those that are medically compromised tend to be those that are marginalised. Very much related to this book's focus is the reported rise of domestic violence and abuse of women and children, that has come with lockdowns and quarantines. While the temptation is to turn our focus away from the social problems well articulated by the authors in this book in order to attend to the health threats, as psychoanalysts and social scientists we must stay alert to the impact of the threat of disease on the mind and the social fabric. *Psychoanalytic and Socio-Cultural Perspectives on Women in India: Violence, Safety, and Survival* is a meaningful contribution that continues to have relevance even in pandemic times.

Conclusion by Gertraud Schlesinger-Kipp

I would like to quote Andreas Bilger, who spoke about the Kolkata conference 2018 at the conference of the German Psychoanalytical Association: "The

International Conferences of COWAP, the Committee of Women and Psychoanalysis of the IPA, is a platform for exchange on the life and social conditions of women worldwide and in different cultural environments. The aim is to strengthen the human dignity and rights of women, to promote psychoanalysis and psychoanalysts and to inspire new ones and support them in their training and development."

We assume that psychoanalysis, with its free and emancipated image of women and men and its development model, is particularly suitable and obliged to develop and protect the rights and needs of people, individuals, and communities, as a form of science and therapy, in questions of the mental and social development of children and young people, of gender roles woman and man, interpersonal relationships, sexualities, respect for other people, cultures, and ideas of life within the framework of generally valid human rights.

In India, there is a long psychoanalytical tradition, but the meeting of the Committee on Women and Psychoanalysis of the IPA is the first international IPA conference in Kolkata, after a COWAP conference 2003 in Mumbai, the second in India.

The topics of society and gender mean that COWAP conferences are planned in an interdisciplinary way and often shed light on the concrete social reality in a more direct and committed way than we are used to at 'normal' conferences. Psychoanalysts, linguists, cultural scientists, and committed activists will shape the lectures and discussions. In India, there are long-established women's and gender movements, which are present and represented in different ways in the public sphere. In India in March 2018, all newspapers during the week of the World Women's Day (8.3.18) were richly filled with women-related reports and feminist activities, encouragement, and illustrations. Just after the conference at the end of August 2018, the news came that India has abolished §377 – punishability of homosexual love – and with it persecution and violence. If you think of the meeting in Kolkata, the colleagues from universities and politics and the committed voices and well-founded statements of gender activists from different social and scientific areas, then you know how much these activities are necessary, helpful, and successful, and how much they contribute all over the world to make societies and the coexistence of human beings more peaceful and to prevent suffering, violence, and injustice. A colleague from India wrote: "Yes, it's deep liberation and celebration time here in India! We feel more hopeful about this country and democracy!" (Andreas Bilger, Tagungsband of the German Psychoanalytic Association, November 2018, translated by GS).

Now we had a second COWAP Conference in Kolkata only a year after the first one and this time completely self-organized. In my long years in COWAP I never met such a resonance and activity in an upcoming IPA society and country like in Kolkata. I met again the enthusiasm, the concentration of researchers and activists form all scenes and parts of the society, and a most interested and psychoanalytic educated audience.

After this, the COVID-19 pandemic and a terrible thunderstorm hit Kolkata so badly that no one knows what happened to all the colleagues, friends, and participants of the two conferences. I hope we will all survive and be able to meet and to work together again.

Index

For Product Safety Concerns and Information please contact our EU
representative GPSR@taylorandfrancis.com
Taylor & Francis Verlag GmbH, Kaufingerstraße 24, 80331 München, Germany

www.ingramcontent.com/pod-product-compliance
Lightning Source LLC
Chambersburg PA
CBHW070350270326
41926CB00017B/4067